Europe Across Boundaries

European History Yearbook
Jahrbuch für Europäische Geschichte

Edited by
Johannes Paulmann in cooperation with
Markus Friedrich and Nick Stargardt

Volume 22

Europe Across Boundaries

Edited by
Noëmie Duhaut and Johannes Paulmann

ISBN 978-3-11-072814-9
e-ISBN (PDF) 978-3-11-077623-2
e-ISBN (EPUB) 978-3-11-077632-4
DOI https://doi.org/10.1515/9783110776232

This work is licensed under the Creative Commons Attribution-NonCommercial-NoDerivatives 4.0 International License. For details go to https://creativecommons.org/licenses/by-nc-nd/4.0/.

Library of Congress Control Number: 2022943354

Bibliographic information published by the Deutsche Nationalbibliothek
The Deutsche Nationalbibliothek lists this publication in the Deutsche Nationalbibliografie; detailed bibliographic data are available on the Internet at http://dnb.dnb.de.

© 2022 with the authors, editing © 2022 Noëmie Duhaut and Johannes Paulmann, published by Walter de Gruyter GmbH, Berlin/Boston
The book is published open access at www.degruyter.com.

Cover image: © Johannes Paulmann
Printing and binding: CPI books GmbH, Leck

www.degruyter.com

Table of Contents

Noëmie Duhaut
Introduction: Writing European History in 2022 —— 1

Richard Herzog
Temporality, Narrative Structure and Strategy in the Works of Two Nahua Scholars, Fernando de Alva Ixtlilxochitl and Domingo de Chimalpahin —— 9

Samuel B. Keeley
"Will the Day Break in the East?": The Origins of Anglo-Prussian Protestant Bishopric in Jerusalem, 1840–1880 —— 37

Sara Müller
Trading and Invading: The Kaiserin-Augusta-River-Expedition and its Collecting Strategies in German New Guinea —— 63

Tom Menger
Of "Golden Bridges" and "Big Bags": Thinking the Colonial Massacre in British, German and Dutch Manuals of Colonial Warfare, c. 1860–1910 —— 79

Riley Linebaugh
Protecting Bad Intel in a Dirty War: Britain's Emergency in Kenya and the Origins of the 'Migrated Archives', 1952–1960 —— 99

Forum

Johannes Paulmann
Researching the History of Social Differentiation and Human Categorization —— 123

Biographical Notes —— 143

Noëmie Duhaut
Introduction: Writing European History in 2022

The present issue of the European History Yearbook showcases research initially presented at the annual Mainz-Oxford graduate workshop "European History Across Boundaries from the Sixteenth to the Twentieth Century" over the past few years. Albeit broad, the chronological limits are clear. And so is our approach. This workshop is a forum for doctoral candidates and early career researchers to present work that sheds the straightjacket of national history and crosses boundaries and borders. We do so by discussing the transcultural, transnational, and transimperial scopes of their research. Methodologically speaking, the European history that workshop participants have been researching and writing draws on comparative history, the study of transfer processes and entanglements, and the *histoire croisée*, among others.

What about the geographical scope? What Europe do the workshop participants imagine? How do they conceive of European history? A glance at the table of contents will suffice. Both participants and organisers are not only interested in writing European history across boundaries but also in decentring Europe. Individual papers deal with Central America, East Africa, the Middle East, and Oceania. They take the readers thousands of kilometres away from the imperial metropolises of Berlin, Madrid, or London – and yet still tell a story about these European imperial centres and societies.

Getting away from nationalistic history writing has been the programmatic and political aim of a range of books, starting with *Histoire mondiale de la France* in 2017, followed by a flurry of global histories of Catalonia, Flanders, Germany, Italy, Portugal, Spain, and Sicily. Great Britain is the only Western European country missing in this new history writing exercise.[1] These works seek to ex-

---

[1] Patrick Boucheron et al. (eds.), *Histoire mondiale de la France*, Paris, 2017, translated as *France in the World: A New Global History*, New York 2019); Andrea Giardina and Emmanuel Betta (eds.), *Storia mondiale dell'Italia*, Bari 2017; Xosé M. Núñez Seixas (ed.), *Historia mundial de España*, Barcelona 2018; Giuseppe Barone (ed.), *Storia mondiale della Sicilia*, Bari 2018; Borja de Riquer, Joaquim Albareda i Salvadó, and Josep M. Salrach i Marés (eds.), *Història mundial de Catalunya*, Barcelona 2018; Marnix Beyen (ed.), *Wereldgeschiedenis van Vlaanderen*, Kalmthout 2018, translated into French as *Histoire mondiale de la Flandre*, Wateloo 2020; Andreas Fahrmeir (ed.), *Deutschland: Globalgeschichte einer Nation*, Munich 2020; C. Fiolhais, José Eduardo Franco, and José Pedro Paiva (eds.), *História global de Portugal*, Lisbon 2020, translated into English as *The Global History of Portugal: From Pre-History to the Modern World*, Brighton 2022; Quentin

plore the past from a perspective and within an analytical framework that go beyond the geographical unit in question, be it a state or a region. While they were editorial successes among non-academic audiences, one can wonder how successful they were in decentring national history. As others have pointed out, by taking a given state or region as a starting point, one runs the risk of writing a history of its influence on the world or reinforcing artificial distinctions between this geographical unit and the rest of the world.[2]

The novelty of this historiographical approach is also questionable. Historians of empire are used to thinking globally: they have long been deconstructing the colonial gaze and investigating how imperial expansion impacted metropolitan societies.[3] The contributions in this issue of the *European History Yearbook* are yet another proof that, for an emerging generation of historians, it is inconceivable to write European history without thinking about empire or to separate the history of Europe from its global and imperial dimensions.[4] Animated by a desire to look at European history from the viewpoint of its overseas empires, the authors in this issue share several interests. In what follows, we briefly outline the most salient threads that run through their articles.

Knowledge, Information Control and Archives

Although separated by three centuries and one ocean, Richard Herzog and Riley Linebaugh's pieces resonate with one another. They explore a central feature of colonial rule – that of knowledge and information control. Both papers tell us about archives, their ownership, and history writing in colonial and post-colonial contexts. Whether in the case of twentieth-century British-controlled

---

Deluermoz (ed.), *D'ici et d'ailleurs: histoires globales de la France contemporaine (XVIIIe–XXe siècle)*, Paris 2021.
2 For critical takes on this new trend, see Arthur Asseraf, 'Le monde comme adjectif: retour sur l'*Histoire mondiale de la France*', in: *Revue d'histoire moderne & contemporaine* 68, no. 1 (2021), 151–162 and Pol Dalmau and Jorge Luengo, 'Historia global e historia nacional: ¿una relación insalvable?', in: *Ayer* 120, no. 4 (2020), 311–324.
3 Ann Laura Stoler and Frederick Cooper, 'Between Metropole and Colony: Rethinking a Research Agenda', in: Ann Laura Stoler and Frederick Cooper (eds.), *Tensions of Empire: Colonial Cultures in a Bourgeois World*, Berkeley 1997, 1–53; Catherine Hall, *Civilising Subjects: Metropole and Colony in the English Imagination, 1830–1867*, Oxford 2002. For a more recent example, see and Sathnam Sanghera, *Empireland: How Imperialism Has Shaped Modern Britain*, London 2021.
4 Gary Wilder, *The French Imperial Nation-State: Negritude & Colonial Humanism between the Two World Wars*, Chicago 2005. For a recent general history of Europe, see Johannes Paulmann, *Globale Vorherrschaft und Fortschrittsglaube: Europa 1850–1915*, Munich 2019.

Kenya or early-seventeenth-century Spanish Mexico, the colonial power forcibly moved archives concerning the colony to the metropole. As Herzog reminds us, archives are knowledge repositories. Shaping their content and making them inaccessible to colonised populations was a crucial component of colonial rule. It continued to form the backbone of former colonial powers' attempts to control their legacy following decolonisation. Thus, the chronicles of noble indigenous Nahua scholars from the early seventeenth century that Herzog discusses were published only several centuries later. In a similar vein, Great Britain declassified the records concerning the Kenya Emergency of the 1950s that Linebaugh draws on in her research only in the early 2010s. Writing about the Warsaw Jewish Ghetto during the Second World War, Samuel Kassow poignantly described archive making as an act of resistance in front of annihilation. The question he chose for his book title, "Who will write our history?," applies to many other historical contexts.[5] The question of the agency of the native, marginalised, and subaltern in writing their history and how to excavate their voices in archives created by those marginalising and oppressing them is indeed a prominent one – in the field of colonial history perhaps more than in any other field.[6]

Agency in Colonial Contexts

Richard Herzog's paper explores native agency in most depth. His analysis of writings by native scholars who belonged to local elites, who sometimes wrote in the coloniser's language and incorporated elements of its religion, stresses the importance of class when dealing with questions of agency under colonial rule. It also charts strategies of adaptation and compromise – which Homi Bhabha famously described as hybridity – that often characterise situations of unequal intercultural contact.[7] Although focusing on different topics, the contributions by Riley Linebaugh and Sara Müller also point to strategies of local resistance to colonial rule and seek to write locals back into the story they are telling us. Müller's paper demonstrates that current debates over the restitution of spoliated artefacts and works of art often fail to examine the role of local colonised people in acquisition processes – from passive cooperation in the

---

[5] Samuel D. Kassow, *Who Will Write Our History? Rediscovering a Hidden Archive from the Warsaw Ghetto*, London 2009.
[6] Ann Laura Stoler, *Along the Archival Grain: Epistemic Anxieties and Colonial Common Sense*, Princeton 2009.
[7] Homi K. Bhabha, 'Culture's In-Between', in: Stuart Hall and Paul du Gay (eds), *Questions of Cultural Identity*, London 1996, 53–60.

form of forced labour to resistance to it. As Linebaugh points out, the British Colonial Government's obsession with information control was an indication of the precarity of colonial rule, a situation that informants from the ranks of the colonised population could use to advance their own interests.

Transimperial Translations and Cooperation

Another theme that cuts across most papers is the translation of information between imperial dominions and centres. Sara Müller's analysis of the collection process of a shield from the Göttingen ethnological collections tackles this question. How was information on the exact origin and acquisition process lost between the moment the shield was collected in German New Guinea and today? What role did scientific and lay members of expeditions to this colony play in shaping the information available to twenty-first-century researchers? As Müller stresses, acquisition stories are not simple ones. Indeed, she tells us a gripping and unexpected tale of a ship captain who perhaps intentionally let rats wreck the scientists' cataloguing efforts to alter the commercial value of collected artefacts. Tom Menger and Samuel B. Keeley show that information and knowledge did not circulate only between empire and metropole but also between empires. Information routes sometimes went via Europe and sometimes bypassed the continent. Keeley's study of German-speaking church leaders points to another aspect of transimperial cooperation. What we label transimperialism can also be seen from the perspective of language and analysed as, in this specific case, Germanophone imperialism.

The contributions by Keeley, Menger and Müller all underscore the heterogeneity characterising and sometimes hampering European imperialism. Stances on how colonial expansion should be carried out and colonial rule exercised were highly varied. Dissensions between Europeans on the ground – military personnel, commercial, and scientific actors – and state authorities back in Europe are a recurrent feature of imperialism. How should colonial expansion proceed? How should colonial rule be exercised? Who should be in charge in the colonies – civil or military authorities? Such questions were often bones of contention between different actors who depicted themselves as imperial pioneers to gain legitimacy and saw the empire as an opportunity to expand their power at the expense of others.

As Menger reminds us, examining transimperial cooperation and knowledge transfer is essential if one wants to deexceptionalise and decentre individual empires. The history of Europe and the idea of Europe are often written from the perspective of present-day European integration. The creation of the European

Community in the 1950s encouraged a search for common heritage.[8] The vast literature on the topic often constructs a genealogy that places the European Union into a longer tradition of liberal visions. As a result, overviews of the European idea in the nineteenth century mainly focus on liberal pan-European projects. This tendency discards anti-liberal visions that contradict contemporary conceptions of European integration as a project based on political and economic freedom.[9] Studies such as Menger and Keeley's, focusing on cooperation across imperial lines between different European states, are an important reminder that imperial expansion and colonial domination were also shared European projects.[10]

Heterogeneity and Dissonance in Imperial Pursuits

Importantly, by looking at transimperial cooperation, these two authors put on the map countries that feature only too rarely in studies of European colonialism: nineteenth-century Prussia and Switzerland (along with Great Britain) in the case of Keeley's research and twentieth-century Germany and the Netherlands (again, along with Great Britain) in Menger's work. In doing so, they underline the diversity of imperial actors, whose lives crisscrossed states, empires, continents, languages, and sometimes confessions. For instance, Samuel B. Keeley follows the steps of a priest born in a French-speaking family in Switzerland, who converted from Calvinism to Anglicanism, and worked as a missionary in Egypt and Abyssinia for some years before becoming a bishop in Palestine. This biographical approach – present to varying degrees in all the contributions in this issue – allows him to bring individual agency back into history. By priori-

---

8 Gavin Murray-Miller, 'Civilization, Modernity and Europe: The Making and Unmaking of a Conceptual Unity', in: *History* 103, no. 356 (2018), 418–433, here 418.
9 Dieter Gosewinkel (ed.), *Anti-Liberal Europe: A Neglected Story of Europeanization*, New York 2015.
10 Hartmut Kaelble, 'Representations of Europe as a Political Resource in the Early and Late Twentieth Century', in: *Comparativ. Zeitschrift für Globalgeschichte und vergleichende Gesellschaftsforschung* 22, no. 6 (2012), 11–20, here 11; Hayden White, 'The Discourse of Europe and the Search for a European Identity', in: Bo Stråth (ed.), *Europe and the Other and Europe as the Other*, Bern 2000, 67–86. For an attempt to reintegrate colonialism as a constitutive element of European integration in the twentieth century, see Fabian Klose, 'Europe as a Colonial Project: A Critique of Its Anti-Liberalism', in: Gosewinkel (ed.), *Anti-Liberal Europe*, 47–71 and Elizabeth Buettner, *Europe after Empire: Decolonization, Society, and Culture*, Cambridge 2016.

tising people over institutions or discourse and focusing on collective rather than individual biographies, the authors in this issue can zoom in on the role of experience in fashioning ideas and chart paths not taken.[11] In other words, their fine-grained approach restores the complexity and diversity of imperial rule.

Taken together, the contributions of this issue illustrate the broad spectrum of types of imperial rule and imperial rule formation. Müller's paper shows that scientific expeditions consolidated territorial control in an already existing colony, while Herzog's piece highlights how Catholicism helped strengthen Spanish colonial rule in Mexico. Keeley's work focuses on informal imperialism and uses the example of the Jerusalem bishopric to explore the role of religious institutions in advancing claims in a city where virtually every European power sought to have a foothold – most often through religious or caritative institutions.[12] Menger and Linebaugh both underscore the centrality of extreme violence in expanding and maintaining colonial power.

Finally, while the contributions dealing with twentieth-century history in this issue say little about the role of religion in imperial expansion, readers interested in this topic will find ample food for thought in the two articles dealing with earlier periods. Richard Herzog's work discusses how Christian and indigenous conceptions of time differed but also impacted one another. Both his and Samuel B. Keeley's examination of how Protestant imperialism sought to counter and become as global as Catholic imperialism offer a close reading of the ways in

---

[11] I am here indebted to Lyndal Roper's concluding comments at the 2021 Mainz-Oxford graduate workshop. A biographical approach, whether individual or collective, has proved extremely fruitful in the last few years. Among others, it made it possible to chart the exclusion of women from professional politics in modern times. See Glenda Sluga, *The Invention of International Order: Remaking Europe after Napoleon*, Princeton 2021. Through a collective biography of émigré communities, Faith Hillis foregrounded the importance of encounter, practice, and intimacy in the making and unmaking of emancipatory politics in modern European history. Faith Hillis, *Utopia's Discontents: Russian Émigrés and the Quest for Freedom, 1830s-1930s*, New York 2021. Other scholars have similarly brought collective biography to bear on intellectual history, thereby underscoring the multiple affiliations of nineteenth-century national actors. See, for instance, Dominique Kirchner Reill, *Nationalists Who Feared the Nation: Adriatic Multi-Nationalism in Habsburg Dalmatia, Trieste, and Venice*, Stanford 2012 and Konstantina Zanou, *Transnational Patriotism in the Mediterranean, 1800–1850: Stammering the Nation*, Oxford 2018. Recent studies adopting a biographical approach to tease out the transnational and transimperial dimensions of North African history include M'hamed Oualdi, *A Slave between Empires: A Transimperial History of North Africa*, New York 2020 and Jessica M. Marglin, *The Shamama Affair: Contesting Citizenship across the Mediterranean*, Princeton 2022.

[12] For a recent study of informal imperialism, see David Todd, *A Velvet Empire: French Informal Imperialism in the Nineteenth Century*, Princeton 2021.

which missionary activities contributed to imperial expansion and functioned on a day-to-day basis.

As all contributions printed below show, writing European history calls for the crossing of boundaries and borders. As a dynamic space of communication and transfer, "Europe" clearly transcends states, empires, and nations within the continent and in a global world. In recent years, historical research has taken up this challenge and has increasingly paid more attention to such transcultural and transnational dynamics, bringing forward a reflexive understanding of historical processes. This research has also demonstrated the significance of imperial dimensions in the construction and imagination of Europe and, thereby, of asymmetries and hierarchies built into European affairs. This is the focus of the work showcased here. Crossing borders results in new boundaries within and between entangled societies. The control of information and historical knowledge has been affected by this as well as by the agency of colonised and colonisers. By decentring our perspective, the authors bring out transimperial translation and cooperation while considering the heterogeneity and dissonance in imperial pursuits. Above all, the essays demonstrate that we cannot juxtapose Europe or one of its nations and the world. The history of Europe cannot be separated from its imperial dimension – indeed, neither can its present be understood without its imperial past.

Richard Herzog
Temporality, Narrative Structure and Strategy in the Works of Two Nahua Scholars, Fernando de Alva Ixtlilxochitl and Domingo de Chimalpahin

Abstract: *The article focuses on notions of time and narrative structure of the Nahua of central Mexico, as well as their colonial-era reshaping through European influences. These notions are analysed via writings of the major Nahua scholars Fernando de Alva Ixtlilxochitl and Domingo de Chimalpahin, working in the early seventeenth century. They point to the colonial transmission of the Nahua calendar and of Mesoamerican temporalities. In decades of meticulous work, the two authors succeeded in creating new ways of writing history that integrated traditions from both Europe and Mesoamerica and shaped their narrative voices. Both Alva Ixtlilxochitl and Chimalpahin navigated multiple knowledge systems in exceptional ways, and were particularly influenced by their respective indigenous states and by different religious orders. Both wrote against the progressing destruction of Nahua sources and in face of the threat of looming oblivion.*

This article deals with indigenous notions of time and narrative structure, as well as their colonial reshaping through European notions. The main focus throughout is on the Valley of Mexico in present-day central Mexico in the early seventeenth century and specifically on the Nahua, the dominant ethnic group there when the Spanish first arrived. It is from this Mesoamerican region that we have the largest corpus of indigenous historical works in the Americas. The Nahua are better known by the anachronistic name "Aztecs", whereas here we follow the term "Nahua", which is widely used in research, after the indigenous language Nahuatl, then predominant in the Valley of Mexico. Unlike in Europe, for the Nahua – as for many other indigenous groups – time and space were inseparable and therefore politically grounded in cosmological structures. Time was also fundamentally political for the Nahua, as calendars served as the basis for the historiography of each dynastic state.[1] The political upheavals fol-

---

1 Federico Navarrete Linares, 'Chimalpain y Alva Ixtlilxóchitl, dos estrategias de traducción cultural', in D. A. Levin Rojo and F. Navarrete Linares (eds.), *Indios, mestizos, y españoles: Interculturalidad e historiografía en la Nueva España*, Mexico City 2007, 97–112, here 92.

OpenAccess. © 2022 the author(s), published by De Gruyter. This work is licensed under the Creative Commons Attribution-NonCommercial-NoDerivatives 4.0 International License.
https://doi.org/10.1515/9783110776232-002

lowing the Spanish arrival were thus closely accompanied by transformations in conceptions of time.

Our guides to this place and time will be two major Nahua scholars writing their histories in the seventeenth century: Fernando de Alva Ixtlilxochitl (ca. 1578–1650) and Domingo de Chimalpahin (1579–ca. 1660). Both came from noble Nahua families, and their family properties and rights were central to their concerns. Compared to most other indigenous scholars, they thus shared a clear self-portrayal as indigenous nobles. They differed however in writing language and genre: while Fernando de Alva Ixtlilxochitl wrote his chronicles in Spanish, Domingo de Chimalpahin wrote mostly in Nahuatl in the style of the *xiuhopuhalli* or yearly account. This language choice had much to do with their respective audiences and differing social backgrounds. One of Alva Ixtlilxochitl's main intentions was to defend his family's rule over a community facing colonial authorities, for whom Spanish was the main language of official communication. In contrast, for Chimalpahin, transmitting his ancestors' culture and thus keeping it alive was a more pressing concern, making Nahuatl his weapon of choice. Both scholars' massive works were only published from the nineteenth century onwards. By the late sixteenth century, the Spanish Crown had forbidden and actively suppressed writings concerned with native American belief systems in order to aid the Spanish conversion efforts. This made the conservation of indigenous sources an extremely difficult and risky endeavour, tragically hastening their loss; it also meant that almost no native author from Spanish America was published in their own time.[2] By necessity then, this article is also about Chimalpahin's and Alva Ixtlilxochitl's relationship vis-à-vis the colonial power structures and about their strategies of resistance and accommodation.

Both men lived in Mexico City, the administrative centre of the Viceroyalty of New Spain – one of the first truly global cities that functioned as a linking point between Spanish possessions in South America, Asia and Europe. Both incorporated European and Mesoamerican temporalities in different ways that underlie the structures of their history writings and their worldviews. The comparative view of both provides an important perspective on their religious beliefs and their intentions for recording their ancestors' pasts, as well as on the interplay between the two. Before diving deeper into these processes, a brief overview over how temporal notions changed for the Nahua from pre-Hispanic to colonial

---

[2] Arndt Brendecke, 'Der 'oberste Kosmograph und Chronist Amerikas': Über einen Versuch der Monopolisierung von historischer Information', in: Frank Bezner (ed.), *Zwischen Wissen und Politik: Archäologie und Genealogie frühneuzeitlicher Vergangenheitskonstruktionen*, Heidelberg 2011, 353–374, here 365–368.

times is necessary and preceded by a few words on terminology. The terms "Europeans" and "Nahua" are not meant to suggest self-contained cultural groups. After all, the Nahua were by no means a homogeneous group, but rather a wide variety of states linked by a complex system of alliances, enmities and tribute relations. At the same time, Europeans in Spanish America came from a diverse range of Spanish possessions in Europe, including parts of today's Netherlands and Italy, as well as from regions that were not subject to the Spanish Crown.[3] For the sake of simplicity, therefore, we speak here of Europeans and Nahua as a conceptual distinction. Depending on the context, we sometimes also speak of "Spaniards" or, in the religious sphere, of "Christians". In addition, "temporality" is understood here as original time, in other words as an extra-linguistic system of time concepts or relations to time.[4]

According to Ross Hassig, Western scholars have tended to associate Europeans with a linear understanding of time and Mesoamericans with a cyclical one.[5] In the West change is understood to be continuous and cumulative, but not repetitive. In linear time, the past is distinguished from the present, which in turn is different from the future – building on religious ideas of beginnings and endings and developed into the concept of progress during the Enlightenment. At the same time, highly influential thinkers including Aristotle and Newton believed in absolute time: according to them, it was possible to unambiguously measure a time interval between two events, independent of who measured it. In this view, time was independent of and separate from space.[6]

In contrast, Mesoamericans understood events as part of a larger, regularly recurring pattern. In cyclical understandings, time changes in real but endlessly repetitive ways. In other words, we can know there is change when we observe ageing and death; but these "are subsumed under a larger, endlessly repetitive temporality in which fundamental conditions are unchanging in the long

---

[3] Henry Kamen, *Golden Age Spain*, London 2004, 26–30.
[4] Peter Schlobinski, 'Tempus and Temporality: Time in the Languages of the World', in: *Unimagazin. Journal of the University of Hanover* 3–4 (2012), 20–23, https://www.uni-hannover.de/fileadmin/luh/content/alumni/unimagazin/2012_zeit/netz06_schlobinski.pdf (2021–10–14).
[5] Ross Hassig, *Time, History, and Belief in Aztec and Colonial Mexico*, Austin 2001, 1–2.
[6] Stephen Hawking, *A Brief History of Time. From the Big Bang to Black Holes*, New York 1988, 8–10; Eckhard Kessler, 'Zeitverständnisse in der Philosophie der Renaissance', in: Arndt Brendecke, Ralf-Peter Fuchs, Edith Koller (eds.), *Die Autorität der Zeit in der Frühen Neuzeit*, Münster 2007, 23–48, here 23–26. For a volume on questions of security and the future in Europe, see Christoph Kampmann, Angela Marciniak, Wencke Meteling (eds.), *"Security Turns its Eye Exclusively to the Future": Zum Verhältnis von Sicherheit und Zukunft in der Geschichte*, Baden-Baden 2018.

run."⁷ Time changes therefore on a smaller scale but remains unchanging on a larger one. Actions may have immediate consequences but not in the long run; major events rather have roots in earlier patterns that are repeated in the present. Furthermore, for the Nahua (as for other native American groups) a clear separation between time and space was unfathomable since both were intrinsically linked in their cosmology. Despite these clear divergences in how they related to time, however, according to Hassig, both Spaniards and Nahua simultaneously held different linear *and* circular temporal notions, which were applied in varying contexts. In general, linear time dominated in Europe, but circular time was common, as in other parts of the world, through ritual cycles: including the seasons' centrality to agriculture and the domestic cycle.⁸ The multiple temporal notions would have profound effects on the divergent ways in which Nahua and Spanish writers interpreted the outcome of the fall of Tenochtitlan in 1521.

Before the Spanish landed, the main power in the Valley of Mexico in the early sixteenth century was a federation composed of the Acolhua (with the capital at Tezcoco), the Tepanecs (from Tlacopan) and the then dominant Mexica (of Mexico-Tenochtitlan). The Mexica had become the major power in central Mexico only decades earlier, and their young empire was still expanding when Cortés first arrived in the region in 1519. For pre-colonial central Mexico, we can identify, among other things, religiously used cyclical and more politically integrated, teleological concepts of time. Due to this article's scope, a concentration on some main aspects of these notions is necessary. The Nahua also distinguished between mythical events that were temporally unanchored and clearly dated time, each of which was recorded in different works.⁹ While for the Nahua time in a religious context is inherently cyclical, political authorities emphasised linear aspects of time: both understandings of time complemented each other. In accordance with the more random nature of political events, it was important for each ruler to distinguish himself from his predecessor. The *tlatoque* strategically chose which events were recorded by scribes and why.¹⁰

In the cosmology of the Nahua people, time progressed through five (in some narratives four) world ages or "Suns": earth, wind, fire and water, followed by

---

7 Hassig, Time, History, 3.
8 Ibid., 1–4. For a detailed epistemological examination of the Mexica's worldview based on their concepts of causality, time and space, see also L. Ibarra García, *Das Weltbild der Azteken: Entstehung und Begründung*, Berlin 2016, especially 160–186.
9 Hassig, Time, History, 7–8.
10 Ibid., 61–62; Enrique Florescano, *Memory, Myth, and Time in Mexico: From the Aztecs to Independence*, Austin 1994, here 39–41.

the current and final "Sun of Movement". Each Sun ended with natural disasters that brought about the extinction of humanity – as would the current "Sun of Movement", whose end had already been predicted.[11] Among the Mexica in particular, human sacrifices to the sun god played a central role to keep the sun moving and preserve life, thus postponing the end of the world. Pre-colonial codices provide insights into an understanding of the past, which, however, was not explicitly addressed by any Nahua scribes.[12] In his classic study of historical time in New Spain, Enrique Florescano has emphasised the fundamental change in memory and self-image of the Nahua triggered by the conquest due to the dominance of European historiography.[13] Alongside this change, however, research has also identified major continuities with pre-colonial understandings – in areas such as religious beliefs, closely linked to temporalities.[14]

During the colonial period, in addition to the radical changes in cultural values, political structures and historiography, the introduction of Christian concepts of time also led to epistemological upheavals. The destruction of pre-Hispanic calendars in tandem with the introduction of Christian calendars and church bells transformed the experience of time. In the process, Mexico's calendrical complexity was not immediately replaced; this led to the temporary coexistence of Christian and Nahua calendars, ranging from confrontation to mutual adjustments.[15] This was accompanied by massive cosmological changes in New Spain: from the flat earth disc to the round world; from a possible end of the world to the one certain end, the Second Coming of Jesus Christ (parousia) and the salvation of the faithful; from the manifold gods who were not made of flesh to the Trinity and the saints; and from the Mesoamerican Suns to the various world-ages of the European mediaeval world of ideas.[16]

As has become clear, temporal notions in this era directly relate to complex questions of transcultural influences between different belief systems and cosmologies, to be tackled when relevant. In connection with this, strategic uses

---

11 Miguel León-Portilla, *Aztec Thought and Culture: A Study of the Ancient Nahuatl Mind*, Norman 1990, 6.
12 Florescano, *Memory, Myth*, 228–233.
13 Ibid.
14 Hassig, *Time, History*, 1–2.
15 The Gregorian calendar, which is still valid today, was introduced by Gregory XIII in 1582. The implementation of these regulations, as well as other chronological innovations, was delayed in New Spain, where the Gregorian calendar was initially used mainly to coordinate Easter and other festivals, see Hassig, *Time, History*, 120–127.
16 As Hassig notes, medieval Europeans perceived the world in world ages that replaced each other abruptly and not successively. A parallel to the "Five Suns" is that the Fifth Sun could also end at any time, but within a sun there is an eternal present, ibid., 188.

of the past by the Nahua scholars were of special importance to them as subalterns in the colonial system but also to their own integrity. In many ways, they resisted colonisation by rescuing their respective ancestors' history and culture from oblivion. For this it was necessary to borrow elements from the language of the colonisers as well as symbols and ways of transmitting history: the translation from Nahuatl to Spanish and from the logographic codices to alphabetic writing entailed massive epistemological upheavals. In more general terms, many of these transcultural processes of adaptation and resistance are typical of the strategies employed by colonised populations until today. For one prominent example we will briefly turn to South Asia. Various movements connected with postcolonial studies, including the subaltern studies group starting in the 1980s, theorised how colonised people resisted the British during the Raj, via physical as well as epistemological resistance. In this context Homi K. Bhabha has conceptualised "hybridity" as the creation of new transcultural forms within the contact zone spawned by colonial processes. In his view, studying relations between colonisers and colonised highlights the necessarily mutual construction of their subjectivities, countering any ideas of a supposed hierarchical "purity" of cultures. Instead, for Bhabha cultural identity always emerges from an ambivalent and conflictual space.[17]

Subsequently, Latin American researchers in particular applied such an approach to postcolonial studies of Ibero-America. Decolonial studies have opened up further critical impulses for colonial history.[18] Walter Mignolo, for example, identifies the introduction of European paradigms of knowledge as the beginning of an epistemological hierarchy between Latin America and Europe that continues to this day. He underlines the comprehensive subordination of indigenous symbols and knowledge systems to European ones –and thus a necessary adaptation of pre-Hispanic ways of experiencing the world.[19] Yet, these approaches should be questioned as well. An important criticism of decolonial perspectives – as of postcolonial studies – remains that their epistemological transformation has rarely succeeded in escaping the colonial conditions that they themselves denounce. Elizabeth Monasterios, among others, has proposed an or-

---

17 Nasrullah Mambrol, 'Homi Bhabha's Concept of Hybridity' (April 2016), in: *Literary Theory and Criticism*, https://literariness.org/2016/04/08/homi-bhabhas-concept-of-hybridity/ (2022–02–19).
18 For one important anthology of decolonial approaches, see Carlos A. Jáuregui, Enrique D. Dussel, Mabel Moraña, *Coloniality at Large: Latin America and the Postcolonial Debate*, Durham 2008.
19 Walter Mignolo, *The Darker Side of the Renaissance: Literacy, Territoriality, and Colonization*, 2nd ed. Ann Arbor 2003.

ganic insertion of indigenous or African theoretical considerations into postcolonial and decolonial critiques as a viable antidote to this issue.[20] This paper uses these critical decolonial approaches that provide a radical antithesis to Eurocentric historiography.

Still, in historical research, indigenous historians have often been examined in terms of their ethnicity[21] – an important aspect of their self-identification, but ultimately one among several. At the same time, current scholars still oftentimes wrongly classify writings in Nahuatl as "disorganised" or "unhistorical".[22] Yet, we should rather regard them as indigenous traditions that may appear unusual from a European perspective, in part due to the juxtaposition of different source accounts. Approaches from transcultural studies provide further analytical focus regarding such processes; the concept of transculturation itself having deep roots in Latin American and Caribbean thought.[23]

Another rare different and useful approach has been put forward by Federico Navarrete Linares: he understands the works of some Nahua scholars as a cultural dialogue between indigenous and European traditions (*doble diálogo cultural*), ultimately focusing on their discursive means and strategies. José Rabasa's analyses of the voice or narrative instance of both Nahua scholars are generally in line with Navarrete's interpretation and contribute incisive points. From his perspective, a fundamental difference between the two authors can be grasped on the basis of Mikhail Bakhtin's concepts of monophony and polyphony: Alva Ixtlilxochitl could be seen as more adapted to European historiography, with its voice of a single author (monophony), whereas Chimalpahin juxtaposes several sources following the polyphonic Nahua tradition.[24]

These processes and theoretical approaches will be analysed in more detail in the following sections. Firstly, as a basis for the analysis, we turn to a brief presentation of our two protagonists lives', their different auctorial voices, and the much belated publication of their works. The second section focuses on their uses of voice and narrative structure. In a third section, I gauge the diverse

---

[20] Elizabeth P. Monasterios, 'Uncertain Modernities: Amerindian Epistemologies and the Reorienting of Culture', in: Sara Castro-Klarén (ed.), *A Companion to Latin American Literature and Culture*, Malden 2008, 553–58.
[21] See e.g. Salvador Velazco, *Visiones de Anáhuac: Reconstrucciones historiografías y etnicidades emergentes en el México colonial: Fernando de Alva Ixtlilxóchitl, Diego Muñoz Camargo y Hernando Alvarado Tezozónoc*, Guadalajara 2003, passim.
[22] Cf. e.g. Florescano, *Memory, Myth*, 382–83.
[23] For a foundational study, Fernando Ortiz, *Contrapunteo cubano del tabaco y el azúcar*, Madrid 2002.
[24] Navarrete, 'Traducción cultural', 97–100; Mikhail Bakhtin, C. Emerson (transl.), *Problems of Dostoevsky's Poetics*, Minneapolis 2013, 204–236.

and sometimes overlapping temporal notions that are at play in the works of Alva Ixtlilxochitl and Chimalpahin via two passages: the former's depiction of the creation of the world and the latter's telling of his ancestors' migration to Mesoamerica. This section shifts the focus to their use of different historiographical traditions – starting with the mythical Nahua tale of the Four Suns and then turning to so-called cellular principle. The last section hones in on the importance of cultural transmission to the authors.

Throughout, the focus lies on two connected areas: first on issues of transcultural processes, especially regarding the coexistence of Judeo-Christian end Nahua belief systems. Second on both historians' goal of inscribing their ancestors and their home regions into world history, in an age of early globalisation. Alva Ixtlilxochitl and Chimalpahin have only rarely been studied side by side.[25] This comparative view as well as the focus on temporality and history writing in this article opens up new perspectives on the works of both authors and on their expansive worldviews.

Two Scholars, Two Worlds

Fernando de Alva Ixtlilxochitl (ca. 1578–1650) was the son of the Spaniard Juan Pérez de Peraleda with the noblewoman Ana Cortés.[26] His mother was of mixed Spanish and native descent, so that she was considered a *mestiza* within the colonial *casta* system of social classification. Through his maternal grandmother, Doña Francisca Verdugo, Alva Ixtlilxochitl was directly descended from the highest rungs of both Acolhua and Mexica royalty. He was the second-born son of the family, so that the family's rulership over a native community (or *cacicazgo*) passed to his elder brother Don Francisco de Navas. Because of this, Alva Ixtlilxochitl acted as governor in various native communities from 1612 onwards, on the instructions of the Viceroy: first in Tezcoco, then in Tlalmanalco and Chalco. In 1640 he began working as an interpreter at the General Indian Court of Mexico in Mexico City, a Spanish colonial court that dealt exclusively with complaints by and against indigenous communities and individuals.[27] Alva Ixtlilxochitl's fam-

---

25 For an exception see Navarrete's article on their auctorial voices, see Navarrete, 'Traducción cultural'.
26 Velazco, *Visiones*, 3.
27 Germán Vázquez Chamorro, 'Introducción', in: Fernando de Alva Ixtlilxochitl, *Historia de la nación chichimeca*, ed. by Germán Vázquez Chamorro, Las Rozas, Madrid 2000, 23–24; Jorge Cañizares-Esguerra, *How to Write the History of the New World: Histories, Epistemologies, and Identities in the Eighteenth-Century Atlantic World*, Stanford 2001, 224; see also Richard Herzog,

ily came to rule the municipality of San Juan Teotihuacan as *caciques*, but this led to protracted legal disputes before the colonial authorities. In 1612 and 1643, their right to rule was challenged by local elites; in both cases, Fernando de Alva Ixtlilxochitl obtained its preservation, possibly hoping to pass on the rights to his illegitimate son Juan Alva. After Alva Ixtlilxochitl died on 26 October 1650 his son took legal action against Francisco de Navas and obtained the transfer of the family's rulership to his branch of the family.[28]

During his lifetime, the author did not manage to publish his manuscripts; this would only happen centuries later – as was the case for the majority of native American scholars.[29] I should highlight the negative consequences of Spanish historical policy on Nahua historiography here. With the Royal Ordinance of 1577, the previously more lenient attitude towards indigenous cultures had become far stricter. A special position of Chronicler-Cosmographer of the Indies, created in 1571, had the power to confiscate any writings from then on. This meant that many of the central works written by European friars and their indigenous translators were forcibly transferred to Spain and could only be published centuries later. This included the sprawling corpus of writings assembled over decades by the Franciscan Bernardino de Sahagún with the collaboration of Nahua scholars, as well as an important chronicle written by the Dominican Diego Durán.[30]

Moreover, since as early as 1556, the Council of the Indies – the main administrative institution in Spain responsible for the Spanish overseas possessions in the Americas and the Philippines – was in charge of authorising the publication of any book about the Americas; ten years later, all books "dealing with Indians" required royal permission to be published. These censoring activities reflected the growing need of the Spanish Crown to control information on its overseas territories – information of potentially massive importance for its adversaries. In addition, for Spanish kings including Philipp II, there was a particular danger emanating from pre-Columbian codices: their publication could supposedly im-

---

'Acolhua Past and Novohispanic Merit: Self and Community in Fernando de Alva Ixtlilxochitl's Struggles for a Cacicazgo', in: Nikolaus Böttcher, Stefan Rinke, Nino Vallen (eds.): *Distributive Struggle and the Self in the Early Modern Iberian World*, Stuttgart 2019.
28 Bradley Benton, *The Outsider: Alva Ixtlilxochitl's Tenuous Ties to the City of Tetzcoco*, in: Colonial Latin American Review 23/1 (2014), 50 – 51, FN 8; Vázquez Chamorro, 'Introducción', 23 – 28.
29 An important exception was the immensely successful work of the "Inca" Garcilaso de la Vega from Peru, which was printed in Europe (initially in Portugal and Italy) in the early seventeenth century, see Mignolo, *Darker Side*, 204.
30 Brendecke, *Chronist Amerikas*, 365 – 368.

pinge on matters of Christian faith and thus threaten the all-important campaigns to convert native people to Christianity.[31]

Alva Ixtlilxochitl's Spanish-language works had been published starting in the mid-nineteenth century. Early translated editions into English and French focused on his portrayals of Spanish cruelties, a typical device used as part of the so-called "Black Legend."[32] The Black Legend was a historiographical trend going back to the sixteenth century, wielded by Spain's European opponents to demonise the Spanish empire and counter its then near-hegemonic influence. These translations were followed in the twentieth century by two extensive editions by the influential Mexicanists Alfredo Chavero and Edmundo O'Gorman, which continue to inform his status as the best-known Nahua author today.[33] These editions formed part of Mexicanists' larger publication projects that often went hand in hand with a renewed interest in and instrumentalisation of the region's pre-Hispanic past. Currents within Mexican nationalism – starting prior to but accelerating after the Mexican Revolution from the 1930s onwards – held up the Nahua and above all the Mexica as proof of the nation's exceptional heritage. One such current called *Indigenismo* would contribute to giving the colonial-era chronicles a new, albeit warped lease on life.[34]

In contrast, translations of Domingo de Chimalpahin's massive works from Nahuatl were not undertaken until the late twentieth century. At the same time, many of his central writings, now known as the Codex Chimalpahin, were not rediscovered until the 1980s.[35] These different factors mean that to this day Chimalpahin is less well known, at least among an international readership, and less frequently cited than Alva Ixtlilxochitl, which is also reflected in a smaller body of research on him.[36] In contrast, Chimalpahin – like Alva Ixtlil-

---

31 Birgit Scharlau, 'Tradición y traducción: Momentos de una historiografía híbrida en la América Colonial', in: Robert Folger, Wulf Oesterreicher (eds.), *Talleres de la memoria: reivindicaciones y autoridad en la historiografía indiana de los siglos XVI y XVII*, Münster 2006, 201–224, here 216.
32 On these early editions, including one published by Lord Kingsborough in 1848, see Amber Brian, 'The Original Alva Ixtlilxochitl Manuscripts at Cambridge University', in: *Colonial Latin American Review* 23/1 (2014), 84–101, here 93.
33 Fernando de Alva Ixtlilxochitl, Alfredo Chavero (eds.), *Obras históricas de don Fernando de Alva Ixtlilxochitl*, Mexico City 1891; Fernando de Alva Ixtlilxochitl, Edmundo O'Gorman (eds.), *Obras históricas*, Mexico City 1975–1977.
34 Jerome A. Offner, 'Improving Western Historiography of Texcoco', in: Galen Brokaw, Jongsoo Lee (eds.), *Fernando de Alva Ixtlilxochitl and His Legacy*, Boulder, CO 2014, 24–27, 43–47.
35 On the history of these manuscripts, which also contain texts by Alva Ixtlilxochitl and were found in the possession of the British and Foreign Bible Society Library in England, see Brian, *Original Manuscripts*.
36 Navarrete, 'Traducción cultural', 109–110.

xochitl – is very well recognised in Mexico as a source of national cultural heritage, as evidenced by the elaborate repurchase of the Codex Chimalpahin from England in 2014.[37]

In Fernando de Alva Ixtlilxochitl's works, diverse temporalities are at play, based on his dual roots in European and Nahua traditions. First of all, his works generally follow the deeds of Nahua rulers and nobles in pre-colonial times and in the conquest-era. This brings to mind the bias towards royalty and nobility in European medieval chronicles, pointing to their possible influence on the Acolhua author.[38] It should also be noted that he identified as Christian and was very familiar with writings of various religious orders as well. Then again, the history writings of the Nahua also had a similar focal point on elites. On the other hand, Alva Ixtlilxochitl switches to Spanish sources in his description of the Spanish wars of conquest, which clearly affects his narration: his few writings on the early colonial period read differently from the bulk of his writings on Acolhua history, based on indigenous sources.

Domingo de Chimalpahin was never mentioned by other authors in his own time, so our main source for his biography is the man himself. His large corpus contains enough information to reconstruct the main stages of his life. The historian was born as Domingo Francisco in 1579 in the community Tzacualtitlantenanca in the Amecameca region of Chalco, to the southeast of Mexico City.[39] Chalco had a proud pre-Hispanic past as an influential *altepetl* in the Valley of Mexico since the late thirteenth century. *Altepetl* were ethnic states that can be broadly compared to the Mediterranean city-states; they could vary strongly in size and influence. Chalco's status changed with its conquest by the Mexica in 1465, after which Chalco became a tributary of the Triple Alliance. It seems that Chimalpahin's immediate family came from Chalco's lower nobility, in contrast to Alva Ixtlilxochitl.[40] The annalist would remedy his lack of high noble descent by eventually giving his full name as Don Domingo Francisco de San Antón

---

[37] https://www.eluniversal.com.mx/ciencia-y-salud/ciencia/recuperan-e-investigan-el-codice-chimalpahin (2022–01–04). The codex is now at the *Instituto Nacional de Antropología e Historia*, where it is being digitised via an initiative of the Mexican government. A new English translation of Chimalpahin's work is currently being undertaken there, see http://www.codicechimalpahin.inah.gob.mx/introduccion.php (2022–01–04).

[38] Annegret Richter, *Geschichte und Translation im kolonialen Mexiko: Eine Untersuchung ausgewählter historischer Schriften von Fernando de Alva Ixtlilxochitl, Diego Muñoz Camargo und Hernando Alvarado Tezozomoc*, Berlin 2015, 87–88.

[39] Domingo Francisco de San Antón Muñón Chimalpahin Cuauhtlehuanitzin (ed.), *Las ocho relaciones y el memorial de Colhuacan II*, Mexico City 2003, 249 (below shortened to "*Relaciones II*").

[40] Susan Schroeder, *Chimalpahin & the Kingdoms of Chalco*, Tucson 1991, 10–12.

Chimalpahin Quauhtlehuanitzin after his move to Mexico City. It included the names of his maternal grandfather (Domingo) and of a pre-Hispanic Chalca ruler (Quauhtlehuanitzin).[41] The historian's full name then functioned as a curated biography and genealogy. It connected him to his immediate ancestors' nobility and implied access to the highest rungs of his community's pre-Columbian nobility.[42]

After his childhood in Amacameca, the young Chimalpahin was sent to Mexico City. He arrived at a small church at the early age of 14 and remained there at least until the early 1620s, possibly until the end of his life which remains unknown to us.[43] The gifted youth was appointed overseer (*mayoral*) shortly afterwards. Camilla Townsend suggests that the employment was due to his high erudition; or else to noble relatives, since Chalco's elites maintained family ties with the capital.[44] Both his work for friars at the church and his detailed biblical knowledge shown in his writings make it clear that the author saw himself as Christian, similar to Alva Ixtlilxochitl and to many other elite Nahua. Chimalpahin ultimately stood between the pre-Hispanic Chalco-Amecemeca of his ancestors, to which most of his work was devoted, and the colonial capital of New Spain, where he spent most of his life. What is certain is that the move to Mexico City enabled Chimalpahin to further broaden his perspective beyond his native Chalco.

Voice and Structure

As will be shown in comparison with Alva Ixtlilxochitl, Chimalpahin's works are characterised by different temporal concepts and structures, in the context of his European and Mesoamerican sources. At first glance, the structure of Chimalpahin's main work, the *Ocho relaciones* (hereafter "*Relaciones*"), seems more linear than that of his Acolhua contemporary's work: the *Relaciones* begin with the

---

41 *Relaciones II*, 295–297.
42 Richard Herzog, 'Conferring a Universal Scope to Nahua Political Concepts: An Aim in the Works of Domingo de Chimalpahin (Early 17th Century)', in: Laura Dierksmeier, Fabian Fechner, Kazuhisa Takeda (eds.), *Indigenous Knowledge as a Resource? Transmission, Reception, and Interaction of Global and Local Knowledge between Europe and the Americas, 1492–1800*, Tübingen 2021.
43 Domingo de San Antón Muñón Chimalpahin Quauhtlehuanitzin, James Lockhart, Susan Schroeder, Doris Namala Stanford (eds.), *Annals of his Time*, Stanford 2006, 47; Schroeder, *Chalco*, 13.
44 Camilla Townsend, *Annals of Native America: How the Nahuas of Colonial Mexico Kept their History Alive*, New York 2017, 146–147.

Christian creation story, followed by biblical events up to the birth of Jesus; the subsequent bulk of the writings deals with Nahua history up to the early colonial period, with a main focus on the Chalca and the Mexica. This main section, comprising *Relaciones* three to eight, is clearly oriented towards the Nahua genre known as *xiuhpohualli*. The *xiuhpohualli* record the history of a state and its rulers. The content and genre of the work generally determine the structure of its images: *xiuhpohualli* are often structured on the basis of year signs, which are read from right to left or vice versa. This orientation is evident from Chimalpahin's structure, choice of topics, references to orality and decision to write in Nahuatl.

Compared to Alva Ixtlilxochitl, Chimalpahin is more firmly rooted in pre-colonial historical traditions, comparable, for example, to the Mexica Hernán Tezozomoc or to Tlaxcaltec historiography.[45] At second glance, this distinction between the initial biblical history followed by Nahua history cannot be completely maintained – Chimalpahin rather mixes influences from both cultural spheres in the course of the *Relaciones*. Nonetheless, his work is more clearly based on linear concepts of time than Alva Ixtlilxochitl's, despite the use of Mesoamerican dates.

There is no doubt that Chimalpahin, like Alva Ixtlilxochitl, was a committed Christian who wanted to pass on his faith. However, this did not contradict his main goals, which run through and underlie all his work: the preservation and transmission of the history of his ancestors – and of the different Nahua states more broadly – to future generations faced with the very real danger of falling into oblivion.[46] To prevent this, Mesoamerica could not remain rooted only in the past. Rather, it had to become part of world history, just as it was already a central part of global networks in the seventeenth century, a process that Chimalpahin was acutely aware of.

A comparison with the structure of his Acolhua contemporary's works will be illuminating at this point. According to Navarrete, Alva Ixtlilxochitl's adoption of European narration is marked by his writing in Spanish, but also by his assembling of different sources via his own narrative voice. This can be clearly identified as the authorial narrator known from European literature. An example of this is Alva Ixtlilxochitl's version of the creation of man in the *Sumaria relación*. His narrative voice inserts indigenous stories into the biblical version,

---

[45] José Rabasa, 'In the Mesoamerican Archive: Speech, Script, and Time in Tezozomoc and Chimalpahin', in: José Rabasa (ed.), *Without History: Subaltern Studies, the Zapatista Insurgency, and the Specter of History*, Pittsburgh 2010, 205–229, here 205.
[46] Ibid., 227–29; Townsend, *Annals*, 159–160.

retaining only indigenous elements that can be assimilated to European models. This approach strongly resembles that of Europeans including the Dominican friar Diego Durán and their adaptation of indigenous stories to the Bible. At the same time, Navarrete acknowledges the Acolhua author's unique narrative style, with his genealogy of rulers ranging from pre-Hispanic times on to his own time.[47] Rabasa, on the other hand, emphasises a monophonic narrative style and orientation towards European chronicles for Alva Ixtlilxochitl, especially for his main work, the *Historia*. However, in earlier works such as the *Sumaria relación*, different indigenous voices and sources can still be discerned. In this chronicle, Alva Ixtlilxochitl does indeed insert the Four Suns into a biblical temporality as described above, with references to the Flood and the birth of Christ. But the events themselves refer to a repetition that enables the prediction of future events. The central role of prophecy and his use of Mesoamerican dates together with European dates thus testified to an indigenous temporality and to the inclusion of various Nahua sources.[48]

Even the *Historia* contains numerous subtle references to Nahua beliefs and temporality, as will be shown in more detail below: among others, the main deity *In Tlaque in Nahuaque*, and, more generally, the fact that the chronicle begins with the legend of the Suns. Building on the analyses by Navarrete and Rabasa, it should be noted, on the one hand, that the Acolhua scholar is more integrated into monophonic European ways of writing, especially in direct comparison to Chimalpahin. On the other hand, he retains indigenous narrative elements – above all in the early works, but also in the *Historia* – which are then adapted to the writing practices and knowledge of the Spanish audience.

According to Navarrete, Chimalpahin exercises an authorial function, which, however, does not assume absolute authority, but is rather based on his way of organising different versions of an event. Thus, in the *Memorial breve acerca de la fundación de la ciudad de Colhuacan*, the Chalca author juxtaposes several versions of the emigration of the Mexica from their mythic ancestral home Aztlan without evaluating them. However, one version is highlighted by the fact that it comes last, suggesting that Chimalpahin agreed most with this version.[49] I will discuss a similar method of working with different sources in the following:

---

47 Navarrete, 'Traducción cultural', 103–105; Richter, *Translation*, 85.
48 José Rabasa, 'Voice in Alva Ixtlilxochitl's Historical Writings', in: Brokaw, Jongsoo Lee, *His Legacy*, 189–194; Fernando Alva Ixtlilxochitl, Edmundo O'Gorman (ed.), *Obras históricas*, vol. II, Mexico City 1977, 11–22 (below shortened to "*Obras históricas II*").
49 The three versions of the migration story are by native authors Tezozomoc and Cristóbal del Castillo and the Franciscan Torquemada, with del Castillo's version "having the last word." Navarrete, 'Traducción cultural', 105–108. For the *Memorial breve*, see *Relaciones I*, 72–175.

Chimalpahin placed versions of events from the Bible next to versions of other Christian authors, sometimes intermixed with elements from classical antiquity and with Mesoamerican beliefs.

Diverse Temporalities: From Cosmogony to Migration Narratives

The structure of Alva Ixtlilxochitl's works can be subdivided into three types: the various shorter works on pre-Hispanic history, whose linear structure is reminiscent of the Nahua annals; the *Compendio histórico*, his only work exclusively on the conquest and early colonial period; and, finally the extensive *Historia de la nación chichimeca* (hereafter "*Historia*"), which encompasses Acolhua history as well as the conquest period and thus European and indigenous sources. Furthermore, one can detect references to Nahua beliefs and to cyclical understandings of time behind the chronological presentation of rulers' deeds. Alva Ixtlilxochitl's narrative structure, with its overlapping time levels, can be approached particularly clearly by looking at the introduction to his magnum opus, the *Historia*.

As a basis for this discussion, some background needs adding on the complex issue of the introduction of Christianity in colonial Mexico. In an influential study, Louise Burkhart introduced the concept of a "native" or "Nahua Christianity" in order to emphasise the dialogue and creative synthesis inherent in this religious transformation. This view in turn sets her apart from the earlier focus in research on "syncretism" and its stricter separation between Christian and non-Christian elements.[50] In addition, the importance of transcultural processes has been highlighted: thus Spaniards had above all successfully passed on cultural elements that tied in with older traditions, with Christian priests often aware of these overlaps and using them to aid the conversion efforts. On the other hand, these processes also served pre-colonial beliefs to be passed on and evolve, whereby original concepts and symbols were modified. This "double coding" of signs is neither purely European nor purely pre-Hispanic, but rather

---

[50] Louise M. Burkhart, *The Slippery Earth: Nahua-Christian Moral Dialogue in Sixteenth-Century Mexico*, Tucson 1989, 5–12; Amos Megged, *Exporting the Catholic Reformation: Local Religion in Early-Colonial Mexico*, Leiden 1996, 1–13.

led to new beliefs.⁵¹ This approach will prove to be very helpful in understanding the following examples.

Unlike Castilian chronicles such as the *Primera crónica*, which begins with Genesis,⁵² Alva Ixtlilxochitl starts his *Historia* with the well-known Nahua cosmogony narrative and attributes the beginning of time to a Nahua deity. Moreover, the present is directly linked to the history of the Suns, since the last, fourth age (the Fire Sun) is said to exist until the end of the current epoch, and thus until today. At the same time, Alva Ixtlilxochitl modified and suppressed the mythological elements that are particularly reminiscent of indigenous beliefs and difficult to reconcile with Christian views. The large-scale Spanish persecution and destruction of writings on indigenous beliefs forced him to self-censor. Influenced by Christian conceptions of time, Alva Ixtlilxochitl associated the beginning of the fourth sun with the birth of Christ, in both cases tied to the transition from cyclical to linear time.

A use of indigenous historiographical traditions is noticeable in the first section of the *Historia*. There, the creation of the world is traced back to *Teotloquenahuaque Tlachihualcípal Nemoani Ilhuicahua Tlatcpaque*, whose name Alva Ixtlilxochitl translates as "universal God and Creator of all things, according to whose will all beings live, Lord of Heaven and Hell, etc."⁵³ After the creation of the world, this deity brought into being "the first parents of men, from whom all the rest are descended."⁵⁴ There are parallels here to the supreme Nahua deity *In Tlaque in Nahuaque*, whose name can be translated as "Lord of the Close Vicinity"⁵⁵ or also "the one who is close to everything, close to whom everything is."⁵⁶ According to León-Portilla, this is an active principle that provides the universe with a new foundation after the beginning of each epoch.⁵⁷ The names given to the deity follow a Nahua stylistic device known as *difrasismo*, whereby an idea is expressed with two or more words. These complement each other because they are synonyms or represent related ideas. In these metaphorical formulations, a new meaning can also emerge from both

---

51 Margit Kern, *Transkulturelle Imaginationen des Opfers in der Frühen Neuzeit: Übersetzungsprozesse zwischen Mexiko und Europa*, Berlin 2013, 108–132.
52 Alfonso X., Ramón Menéndez Pidal (ed.), *Primera crónica general: estoria de España que mandó componer Alfonso el Sabio y se continuaba bajo Sancho 4 en 1289*, Madrid 1906, fol. 4.
53 Fernando de Alva Ixtlilxochitl, *Historia de la nación Chichimeca*, Barcelona 2011, 19.
54 Ibid.
55 León-Portilla, *Aztec Thought*, 91.
56 Ángel Garibay Kintana, *Poesía náhuatl*, Mexico City 1964, 408.
57 León-Portilla, *Aztec Thought*, 91.

words or their meaning can even be increased, which applies to the supreme deity described here.[58]

Then again, the passage is reminiscent of the Christian creation of the world and human beings by a deity. With the "universal God" and "Lord of Heaven and Earth", Alva Ixtlilxochitl uses designations for the Christian God, in terms that were clearly recognizable for European readers. This brings to mind techniques used by the Franciscans, who would regularly translate central Christian terms such as God, devil and hell into Nahuatl, even when they had no clear counterpart in Nahua cosmology.[59] The Acolhua chronicler was well acquainted with Franciscan writings and would have been aware of such conversion strategies.

Among the various epithets of the creator-god are the "Lord of Creation" mentioned by Alva Ixtlilxochitl, but also synonyms for the deities Tetzcatlipoca[60] and Ometeotl. Both were used interchangeably by the Nahua for *In Tloque in Nahuaque* and are interestingly omitted in Ixtlilxochitl's Spanish translation of the names. This was a common translation strategy he used and that we will encounter again: especially in his main work, the *Historia*, he would sometimes leave out ideas that might be too reminiscent of pre-Hispanic beliefs for his Spanish audience. After all, writings on native spirituality had been forbidden by the Spanish crown since the 1570s. Moreover, the creation of the first humans is attributed to divine intervention in its oldest surviving version in the *Historia de los mexicanos por sus pinturas*, which is dated to the 1530s and thus still appears to follow Nahua traditions closely.[61] Origin myths generally played a central role in the Nahua's self-image, as described above. Accordingly, echoes of Alva Ixtlilxochitl's cosmogony narrative can be found in indigenous and Christian traditions, even if in his case it is clearly identified with the Nahua deity of creation. We can note here how transcultural translation processes were at play during this still formative stage of a Nahua Christianity, with elements present in two different population groups more likely to be passed on.

A similar process is at play in certain passages related to time in Chimalpahin's oeuvre. The work with different types of sources is at the root of a striking

---

58 Diphrase Herkunft, Eigenschaften und Beispiele, in: *Thpanorama*, https://de.thpanorama.com/blog/literatura/difrasismo-origen-caractersticas-y-ejemplos.html (2022–02–10).
59 Burkhart, *Slippery Earth*, 51–53.
60 Toltec and Mexica deity, lord of heaven and earth (Alva Ixtlilxochitl mentions this designation here), source of life, as well as city god of Tezcoco, who is associated with sacrifices and divination, among other things.
61 León-Portilla, *Aztec Thought*, 91–93, 105–106; Leisa Kauffmann, 'Figures of Time and Tribute: The Trace of the Colonial Subaltern in Fernando de Alva Ixtlilxochitl's Historia de la nación chichimeca', in: *The Global South* (2010), 31–47, here 38–39.

feature of his narrative: the simultaneous recording of events that took place in the same year, but often in different places or even on different continents. These include the stories of different *altepetl*, Judeo-Christian history as well as contemporary events in Europe and Asia. In a broader sense, the author is concerned with a revaluation of Mesoamerica and the history of his ancestors in world history, once more in a similar vein to Alva Ixtlilxochitl. In the latter, we find similar juxtapositions of "old-world" and "new-world" events. But this device appears less frequently in the Acolhua author and is used rather to compare individual persons.[62] In contrast, Chimalpahin follows much more closely the model of the *xiuhpohualli* in indicating successive seasons, which creates the impression of a parallel representation of events from several continents.

These precise dates begin in the fourth *relación* with the migration of the Chichimecas to Mesoamerica: "1 *Tochtli xihuitl*, 50 *años*. 50 years after the birth of Jesus Christ, only Son of the true God, Saviour of the world."[63] The Chichimecas as a general term encompasses various groups who invaded central Mexico from the north in the twelfth and thirteenth centuries, ending the earlier Toltec rule; the intermixing between Chichimecas and Toltecs was in turn foundational to all Nahua groups' identities. From this point on, the author can refer to verifiable historical documents – we find here the transition from indeterminate, mythical to determinate and linear time, which for Alva Ixtlilxochitl already begins with the end of the creation story.

Chimalpahin then goes on to record events for a given year in different states, such as Tezcoco, Tenochtitlan and his home state Chalco-Amecameca. This creates a comprehensive picture of the interactions between the *altepetl*, with the Chalca usually receiving the most attention.[64] While in general the other Nahua authors we know largely wrote about their own *altepetl*, especially in the Spanish-language chronicles, other colonial *xiuhpohualli* are known to have depicted the histories of several states as well.[65] Chimalpahin has thus not abandoned the pre-colonial chronology, but rather integrated European dates into it – in a parallel process to his incorporation of biblical events and teachings into his broader history of Mesoamerica. It should be emphasised here that his account of pre-colonial as well as colonial times is grounded in indigenous experiences and records.

---

62 For juxtapositions between Martin Luther, Charles V., Hernán Cortés as well as an ancestor of the Acolhua author, Ixtlilxochitl II, see e.g. Alva Ixtlilxochitl, *Historia*, 24, 161.
63 *Relaciones I*, 307.
64 Rabasa, 'Mesoamerican Archive', 219–220.
65 Navarrete, 'Traducción cultural', 98.

Chimalpahin bases his commentaries on ancient scholars and biblical stories on a Mesoamerican perspective. On the one hand, the author uses these sources in the *Relaciones* primarily to support his argument that the Nahua and their pre-colonial ancestors had recognised God and been redeemed by Him. What is more, he is concerned with their equality within Christian universal history. On the other hand, indigenous structural and linguistic adaptations including oral traditions are also evident in his interpretations of biblical passages. Christian notions of time and history become part of the Nahua tradition of the *xiuhopualli* in Chimalpahin, which now encompasses all known continents – a universal story with its starting point not in Europe but rather in Chalco.

According to Elke Ruhnau, Chimalpahin ultimately wanted to convince his readers that Christianity was in fact nothing other than their pre-Hispanic faith.[66] Moreover, this testifies to the author's will to draw on biblical teachings in order to defend and enhance Nahua history and culture, a clear narrative technique. As Rabasa notes, Chimalpahin thus inscribes his ancestors in Christian universal history, much as the Franciscans had done. Conversely, this means that the world appears in some ways as originally Nahua: "the stories of old survive as remains resulting from the negation yet preservation of ancient spirituality from within the Christian institutions of historical writing. The universal history of Christianity now includes, along with the Roman past, traces of Mesoamerican civilization."[67]

Transcultural History Writing I: The Four Suns and Nahua Providence

Creation is followed in the *Historia* by the story of the Four Suns (or four ages). The *Leyenda de los Soles* of 1558 is a useful point of comparison as the most complete of the more than ten surviving chronicles and annals, as well as probably the oldest version of the narrative, since it goes back to an oral commentary for an indigenous manuscript. Moreover, a version of the *Leyenda* was included in the archive of manuscripts passed on by Alva Ixtlilxochitl, so he was clearly familiar with it.[68] At first glance, several similarities between the two texts are

---

66 Elke Ruhnau, 'Consolidating the Indians' Christian Faith: An Indian Author's Objectives in Writing a Universal History', in: *Journal de la société des américanistes* 84/2 (1998), 197–208, here 198–202.
67 Rabasa, 'Mesoamerican Archive', 228.
68 Rabasa, 'Voice', 192.

striking: the Suns of water, air and fire are found, albeit in a different order, ending each with the appropriate catastrophes (floods, winds and firestorms). Alva Ixtlilxochitl, however, notes for the Sun of Air that the surviving people found monkeys brought to them by the wind, to which the "very falsified fable"[69] about transformations of people into monkeys can be attributed. In contrast, in the *Leyenda*, at the end of three of the four extinct ages, the disappearing humans transform into a species of animal (first into monkeys, then into turkeys and finally into fish).

In contrast, Alva Ixtlilxochitl's dating in his chronicle is very imprecise; he only gives the names of the Suns in Nahuatl.[70] In his *Sumaria relación de todas las cosas que han sucedido en la Nueva España* he gives more precise Nahua dates for the epochs and their demises, so we can assume that in the *Historia* these are not unknowing but deliberate omissions of the pre-Hispanic chronological system. We have seen him use a similar technique when translating the various names of the supreme deity, leaving out elements of pre-Hispanic faith. Moreover, in the *Sumaria relación* he states that many legends (*fábulas*) were told by the Toltecs about the people, as in the other countries of the world, which he would omit for the sake of brevity.[71] Such legends may well have been perceived as idolatrous by his Spanish readers, as he knew all too well.

This statement is matched by Fernando Alva Ixtlilxochitl's explanation in the *Historia* of one of the frequent accounts in the *Leyenda* of therianthropy, a central component of Nahua beliefs, in an accessible, rational way to the Spaniards. Therianthropy is a spiritually charged concept denoting the transformation of a human being into an animal or into a being possessing human and animal characteristics. The capacity for animal anthroponomy was particularly attributed to Nahua priests, and the concept continued to have an impact in the colonial period.[72] Alva Ixtlilxochitl's narrative of the Suns is not the only one that does not mention the Fifth Sun, the Sun of movement. The origin of this era, as reproduced by the Franciscan Bernardino de Sahagún, is attributed to the sacrifice of two gods in the major ancient city Teotihuacan, one of whom, Nanahuatzin, was

---

69 Alva Ixtlilxochitl, *Historia*, 19.
70 Ibid., 19–21; León-Portilla, *Aztec Thought*, 37–39.
71 For a graphic and tabular comparison of various versions and their differences, including from the *Historia de los mexicanos por sus pinturas* and the *Popol Vuh*, see Enrique Florescano, 'Los paradigmas mesoamericanos que unificaron la reconstrucción del pasado: el mito de la creación del cosmos; la fundación del reino maravilloso (Tollán), y Quetzalcóatl, el creador de estados y dinastías', in: *Historia Mexicana*, 52/2 (2002), 309–359, here 318–323.
72 Elizabeth Hill Boone, *Stories in Red and Black: Pictorial Histories of the Aztecs and Mixtecs*, Austin 2000, 19.

reborn as the sun. The other gods sacrificed themselves to preserve the sun – the ritual purpose of human sacrifices can be traced to this story. At the same time, for the Mexica these sacrifices ensured the continuation of all life.[73] Restriction to four epochs can thus be traced back to Alva Ixtlilxochitl's sources.

In view of Spanish censorship, this also appears as an attempt to omit the mythical explanation for human sacrifice – the Nahua ritual that was probably most fiercely rejected by the Spanish. After all, the existence of human sacrifice among the Nahua was the main justification Spanish scholars used to legitimise the conquest of their territories by force, presented influentially among others by the humanist Juan Ginés de Sepúlveda. While debates about the "benefits" of indigenous conversion to Christianity were fierce, this argument could generally be countered with little. The extent and actual cosmological significance of these sacrifices, on the other hand, were barely understood in Europe for centuries.[74]

A transcultural process is evident here, whereby Alva Ixtlilxochitl translated Nahua understandings of time and history into Spanish and in a way that the Spanish could understand, thereby saving those notions from oblivion. In the first chapter of the *Historia*, there is a shift from cyclical to linear time, based on both Mesoamerican and Christian temporalities. Models for his approach can be found in the cyclical legend of the Four Suns and in eschatological teachings of the Franciscans as well as in linear historical works of the Spaniards and Nahua. Acolhua history becomes part of universal history in Alva Ixtlilxochitl, without diminishing its vitality and significance.

As we have seen, a quite similar though not identical process was at play in the writings of his contemporary, Domingo de Chimalpahin. Firstly his expositions of biblical teachings are presented, through which he tried to describe a supposed proto-Christianity for the Nahua. Then the focus moves to his less conspicuous Mesoamerican influences in the first *Relaciones*. These are instructive both for his conceptions of time and beliefs, and as a point of comparison with Alva Ixtlilxochitl.

At the very beginning of the first *relación*, the author makes it clear that for him, the Bible reveals a common ancestry of all people, and thus also of the Nahua. According to him, not only indigenous converts to Christianity can be redeemed, but their unbelieving ancestors as well. The pre-colonial Nahua were not destined for eternal damnation but shared in divine salvation – although

---

[73] León-Portilla, *Aztec Thought*, 43–45.
[74] For a recent overview, see Wolfgang Gabbert, 'Human Sacrifice, Ritualised Violence and the Colonial Encounter in the Americas', in: Robert Antony, Stuart Carroll, Caroline Pennock (eds.), *The Cambridge World History of Violence*, Cambridge 2020, 96–116.

Jesus was unknown to them, they lived in him. They had certainly emigrated to the Americas on God's plan and had been led astray by the devil there.[75] Once again, this works as a "Nahuanisation" of Christianity by making the unfamiliar appear more familiar to European eyes. We can also note Franciscan influence here, since the Franciscan Juan de Torquemada had fully developed a complicated narrative of how the devil fleeing God had come to the Americas. Both protagonists of this article were familiar with the works of Torquemada and earlier Franciscan authors, and their influence certainly shines through on multiple occasions.[76]

The interpretation by Chimalpahin clearly contradicts the missionaries' doctrine following which the unconverted ancestors of the natives suffered in purgatory. This view was put forward in the *Doctrina Cristiana* written by the Dominican monk Pedro de Cordoba in Santo Domingo and published in Mexico City in 1544 under the archbishop Juan de Zumárraga.[77] The Chalca scholar thus went even further than the Dominican Bartolomé de las Casas, whose famous defence of the indigenous people continued to be based on the necessity of their conversion. At the same time, Chimalpahin integrated the Christian view common in the sixteenth century, according to which Nahua belief and idolatry went back to Satan, put forward by Bernardino de Sahagún, among others.[78] For Chimalpahin, his own argument had far more at stake than for the monks: the salvation of his family and ancestors, and ultimately that of all the indigenous people whose lives his historical work encompassed. His positionality produced a highly original interpretation of individual Christian views.

Domingo de Chimalpahin's access to European and, above all, biblical history is evident here. Similarly to Alva Ixtlilxochitl, Chimalpahin also draws on multiple indigenous influences in the first *Relaciones*, so that it would be simplistic to describe the work solely as universal history following European scriptural traditions. Since the majority of the *Relaciones* deal with pre-colonial history, it is not surprising that the biblical elements are also ultimately in the service of Nahua history and interests. Thus, it is no coincidence that the first *relación* begins with a lengthy exposition on classical philosophers. This stands in clear contrast to the typical structure of universal histories that begin with the creation of the world. Rather, the author wants to make clear right at the beginning that ancient Greeks, despite their paganism ("[a]ll these idolatrous gen-

---

75 León-Portilla, *Aztec Thought*, 57.
76 Jorge Cañizares-Esguerra, *Puritan Conquistadors: Iberianizing the Atlantic, 1550–1700*, Stanford 2006, 104–110.
77 Ruhnau, 'Universal History', 204; Townsend, *Annals*, 108.
78 Burkhart, *Slippery Earth*, 39–40.

tiles"),⁷⁹ had knowledge of the Christian God – which should thus naturally also apply to the pre-colonial Nahua and their ancestors.⁸⁰ Chimalpahin makes this comparison explicit: according to him, the scholars of European antiquity were pagan priests and yet understood that all sciences come from God, and likewise "we also think that earthly laws concern us as human beings."⁸¹ In this way, the passage skilfully prepares the reader for the numerous examples of divine intervention in Mesoamerican history that run through his work.

More generally, the structure is also reminiscent of indigenous historiography: Chimalpahin does not deal with this divine intervention in a linear fashion but rather elaborates on individual cases in later *Relaciónes*. For example, a mythical emigration narrative about the Chalca's ancestors from Eurasia to Mesoamerica in the year 50 CE is briefly mentioned in the first *relación*; subsequently, the destruction of the temple in Jerusalem directly preceding the emigration (fourth *relación*) and then the emigration itself (seventh *relación*) are treated in more detail. This is in line with the so-called cellular principle of Nahua historiography, wherein individual events are described several times in order to emphasise their great importance.⁸² Moreover, Chimalpahin builds on these principles to in turn juxtapose historical events from both parts of the world and, in the case of the emigration, even to connect them. It is once again the inscription of Mesoamerica and its inhabitants into a world history whose European historians largely ignored them at the time.

At the same time, the Chalca author applied this Mesoamerican structure to biblical stories, which also explains why references to divine intervention in Nahua history run through almost all the *Relaciones*. This allowed him to ensure that his targeted, educated Nahua audience absorbed his central messages. The approach is related to his indigenous sources as well. In the seventeenth century, Chimalpahin could no longer draw directly on the important oral accounts from elders who had lived through the pre-Hispanic period themselves, as earlier Nahua historians had done. Instead, he had to rely on bibliographic documents, transcriptions of oral testimonies and narratives from people who had known

---

79 Domingo Francisco de San Antón Muñón Chimalpahin Cuauhtlehuanitzin, Rafael Tena (eds.), *Las ocho relaciones y el memorial de Colhuacan I*, Mexico City 2003, 35 (below shortened to "*Relaciones I*").
80 Elke Ruhnau, 'The First Relation of Chimalpahin's Diferentes Historias Originales: Its Sources and the Author's Intention', in: *Indiana* 19–20 (2002), 277–287, 10.
81 *Relaciones I*, 33.
82 Camilla Townsend, 'Glimpsing Native American Historiography: The Cellular Principle in Sixteenth-Century Nahuatl Annals', in: *Ethnohistory* 56 (2009), 625–650, passim.

survivors of the wars of conquest and the massively destructive epidemics.[83] Chimalpahin's juxtaposition of several source accounts from different places – with partly differing chronologies – is thus rooted in Nahua historiographical traditions, but also due to the practical limitations of information gathering a hundred years after the arrival of the Spaniards. He ultimately transferred the cellular principle to biblical history as well, with juxtaposed versions from several sources, including Christian authors of the Middle Ages and the Renaissance. This way of working brings to mind the double coding of transculturation, where elements used in both groups are more likely to be transmitted. Chimalpahin, equally at home in both Mesoamerican and European knowledge systems, was able to impressively distil and further develop the historiographical techniques he had learned from his ancestors.

Transcultural History Writing II: Transmission

Rabasa specifically examines connections between the works of Chimalpahin and Hernán Tezozomoc, the important Mexica author and descendant of the Mexica ruler Moctezuma whose *Chronica Mexicayotl* Chimalpahin created a copy of. This relationship is therefore instructive as an additional point of comparison. Tezozomoc is ultimately one – albeit a particularly prominent one – among Chimalpahin's many sources that he incorporated into his work in the manner outlined above.[84] While Rabasa only hints at this, it can be added that both authors show a similar understanding of time with the parallel use of dates from Mesoamerican and European calendars.

Moreover, both emphasise the transmission of the history of their respective ancestors to future generations as a main goal. Tezozomoc's *Chronica Mexicayotl* begins with a declaration of intent to write so that later indigenous inhabitants of his native *altepetl* Mexico-Tenochtitlan (later Mexico City) can learn much about Mexica history.[85] His words echo in the impressive introduction to Chimalpahin's eighth *relación* which underlines the urgency of his intention to pass on the origins and lineage of his home state to its future generations. Chimalpahin was aware of the similar passage in Tezozomoc, having copied the latter's work.

---

83 Rabasa, 'Mesoamerican Archive', 220–221.
84 Ibid., 219–221; Townsend, *Annals*, 153–154.
85 Hernán Tezozómoc, Domingo Francisco de San Antón Muñón Chimalpahin Cuauhtlehuanitzin, Berthold Riese (transl.), *Crónica Mexicayotl: Die Chronik des Mexikanertums des Alonso Franco, des Hernando de Alvarado Tezozomoc und des Domingo Francisco de San Antón Muñón Chimalpahin Quauhtlehuanitzin*, Sankt Augustin 2004, 1–7.

Furthermore, the argumentation of both authors testifies to the survival of the oral tradition to which they directly refer – in the quotation, their own ancestors who created the codices are traced back over several generations. Chimalpahin is only too well aware of the immense responsibility of his project, the failure of which could have well meant the final interruption of an irretrievable and deep running historiographical genealogy from Chalco.[86]

The same concern is also found in Alva Ixtlilxochitl, albeit formulated more indirectly. In the dedication of his *Sumaria relación,* he sharply criticises the Spanish destruction of major native cultural assets and sources: "the greater part of which was burnt in a careless and inconsiderate manner by order of the first clergy, which constituted one of the first damages in this New Spain."[87] Moreover, already in this early work, Alva Ixtlilxochitl presents Tezcoco as the cultural centre of central Mexico. According to this, Tezcoco housed the "royal archives". These would have included all the different types of Nahua sources, which in turn were destroyed by the Spaniards. The documents that were saved from these "calamities and fires" were taken over by the author himself from older nobles.[88] On the one hand, Alva Ixtlilxochitl's intention here, as in the entire dedication, is to enhance his historiography before colonial authorities by underlining his special access to Acolhua sources and his superior knowledge of the Nahuatl language. On the other hand, it is clear from the passage that he was all too aware of the genuinely precarious situation of documenting Tezcoco's history. After all, it was this history that he would record throughout his impressive oeuvre in the greatest detail compared to other authors. Ultimately, he was in the same situation as his contemporary Chimalpahin: both wrote against the progressive destruction of Nahua sources and in face of the threat of looming oblivion.

Concluding Remarks

The dual analysis of the first chapter of Alva Ixtlilxochitl's *Historia* and of Chimalpahin's first *Relaciones* has revealed individual differences, but also important similarities between the two. The differences are above all structural. The use of different languages is directly related to their respective genres and target audiences: Alva Ixtlilxochitl's Spanish-language chronicle is initially aimed at

---

86 Townsend, *Annals*, 158.
87 *Obras históricas II*, 18.
88 Ibid.

the Spanish colonial administration, mostly following European monophony. In contrast, Chimalpahin's polyphonic work is much more oriented towards Nahua historiography; only the writing language (Nahuatl) indicates his intended indigenous audience. The very different success of the two writers in modern times is ultimately also due to their different choices of language and narration: while Alva Ixtlilxochitl, published since the late nineteenth century, is probably the best-known Nahua author in Mexico and outside Mexico today, Chimalpahin's importance has only become more widely recognised with the later increasing editions of his works, especially since the late twentieth century.[89]

Apart from these differences, often noted in research, major parallels must also be emphasised. Both scholars were convinced Christians, which is reflected in their works. The influence of a transformed "Nahua Christianity" shines through as well, which was not an exact transfer from Europe to America – numerous references to native cosmology testify to this. These allusions, in combination with the parallel use of European and Mesoamerican dates, point to the colonial transmission of the Nahua calendar and thus also, at least to some extent, of Mesoamerican temporalities. These are not just isolated remnants of pre-Hispanic culture. The elements depicted rather are a central component of Nahua cosmology to whose survival both authors contributed together with other native scholars, among them Hernán Tezozomoc and Diego de Muñoz Camargo. This was a determined – if not the central – concern of Chimalpahin and Alva Ixtlilxochitl: they wanted to preserve the rich heritage of their ancestors from the threat of imminent extinction and to pass it on to future generations, along with the stories of their own *altepetl*.

It is important to note here that Christian influences shaped both of them as well as other Nahua authors; but that they integrated the influences into a decidedly Mesoamerican worldview, and not vice versa. A Dominican influence is likely in Chimalpahin's polyphony. As has been shown, however, Chimalpahin's polyphonic structure was based primarily on Nahua historical conventions – in contrast, for example, to Alva Ixtlilxochitl's monophonic and thus Europeanised narrative style which subordinated multiple voices to one authorial voice. The cellular principle underlay Nahua society at all levels, from cosmology to gender roles to politics. Based on this, Chimalpahin often juxtaposes the description of an identical event from multiple indigenous sources or voices without evaluating them. Transculturation has proved to be a useful lens for approaching both scholars' ways of writing that were neither solely Mesoamerican nor solely European.

---

89 Navarrete, 'Traducción cultural', 109–110.

Stepping back from the specific processes, I want to stress the strife and the violence at the root of both scholars' works. As mentioned above, postcolonial approaches have been taken up and critically discussed in Latin American studies. In an influential essay, for example, Carolyn Dean and Dana Leibsohn have questioned the hybridity concept in the context of colonial Spanish America. For them "certain kinds of alterity trouble cultural norms (and, therefore, social or political authorities) in different ways at different moments in history. Further, what does not fit the normative culture opposes, or in some way threatens, the status of the norm. [Hybridity] is necessarily a sign that intolerance was and is at work marking alterity from fixed norms as dangerous to those norms."[90] This view brings into focus the tensions embedded in the two authors' ways of working. On the one hand, both were aware of certain Nahua views that veered too far from the norm, prompting them to make strategic omissions. On the other hand, however, their alterity was and is fundamental: thus, it is no coincidence that Chimalpahin, writing in his own language, has been neglected for centuries.

Clearly the physical violence of colonial rule, as well as the destruction of native sources and knowledge repositories left a long-lasting mark on Nahua historiography. This was accompanied by symbolic violence in writing histories, combined with the performative power to legislate. José Rabasa has explored this "language of violence" in the changing Spanish law codes, including in the representation of the conquest campaigns as "peaceful" colonisation (*pacificación*).[91] In this context, writing is closely linked to power structures; power structures that in turn limit what can be spoken and written about. However, for Rabasa any colonial rule relies on the heterogeneity of subaltern subjects. Thus, power structures do not prevent one from writing about what is the Other and outside the discourses of domination. With Nahua scholars, it is therefore helpful to distinguish between different "regimes of violence" – including the difference between sources intended solely for one's own community and those intended for the colonial authorities.[92] The struggles and the strategies both of our protagonists used thus speak to more widespread dilemmas inherent to colonial hierarchies: how to pass on one's peoples' culture and stories from a position of subalternity – and to whom?

---

90 Carolyn Dean and Dana Leibsohn: 'Hybridity and Its Discontents: Considering Visual Culture in Colonial Spanish America', in: *Colonial Latin American Review* 12/1 (2003), 5–35, here 26–27.
91 José Rabasa, *Writing Violence on the Northern Frontier: The Historiography of Sixteenth-Century New Mexico and Florida and the Legacy of Conquest*, Durham 2000, 6–8.
92 Ibid., 14–15.

In this context, Alva Ixtlilxochitl and Chimalpahin had something else in common: in decades of meticulous work, they both succeeded in creating new ways of writing history that integrated traditions of both Europe and Mesoamerica. Their difference vis-à-vis European chronicles is due to the indigenous background of the authors, their embeddedness in Nahuatl and in Nahua sources. Both navigated multiple knowledge systems in exceptional ways, were particularly influenced by their respective indigenous states and different religious orders, and for this reason cannot be fully understood by European observers then or now.[93] Both worked in an age and a place of creative innovation and unforeseeable crises which informed their singular and striking visions. More generally, the two scholars and ultimately Nahua literature as such not only enrich the historiography of the world – as they themselves noted. They also represent an essential part of its cultural heritage, which reaches far back into the pre-colonial history of Mesoamerica. In other words, the colonial Nahua authors can be understood as one part of a larger and vibrant non-European canon whose components continue to be negotiated.

---

93 José Rabasa, *Tell Me the Story of How I Conquered You: Elsewheres and Ethnosuicide in the Colonial Mesoamerican World*, Ann Arbor 2014, 89–90.

Samuel B. Keeley
"Will the Day Break in the East?": The Origins of Anglo-Prussian Protestant Bishopric in Jerusalem, 1840–1880

Abstract: *This paper examines the origins and motivations behind the foundation of a Protestant Bishopric in Jerusalem in 1840, jointly-run by the British and Prussian states. The Bishopric was intended to be an explicitly missionary institution, in order to convert Jewish people living in Jerusalem to Protestantism. At the same time, it served a geopolitical purpose, as both Prussia and England were interested in having a colonial presence in the Holy Land. For Prussia, in particular, the Bishopric offered a rare and early opportunity to extend their own religious and political footprint far beyond Central Europe. By examining some of the early activities of the Prussian ambassador to England, Christian Carl Josias von Bunsen (1791– 1860), this paper will show that Prussian state officials had explicit and sincere religious motivations in addition to incentives that had to do with geopolitical or national interest.*

> The King had called me in with a view to do something in the Holy Land; and that it might be the will of the Lord, and probably would be that of the King, that in Jerusalem the two principal Protestant Churches of Europe should, across the grave of the Redeemer, reach to each other the right hand of fellowship.[1]

In 1841, the first Protestant Christian Bishopric was established in Jerusalem, to be jointly organized and funded by the Prussian and British monarchies, and ministered by bishops selected alternatingly by both the Anglican and Prussian Lutheran churches. The Jerusalem Bishopric project lasted for over four decades, until Prussia withdrew its involvement in 1886. In theory, the Bishopric was intended to serve the spiritual needs of Protestants living in not only Palestine, but also across Mesopotamia, Egypt, and Syria. In practice, the Bishopric was a beachhead for proselytism in the region, and a bold, early assertion of ascendent Protestantism on the global stage in the middle of the nineteenth century.

This article explores the origins and motivations behind the foundation of this transnational, syncretic Bishopric, by specifically addressing the influence

---

[1] Bunsen to his wife, 26 April 1841, in: Frances Bunsen (ed.), *Memoir of Baron Bunsen: Late Minister Plenipotentiary and Envoy Extraordinary of His Majesty Frederick William IV at the Court of St. James; Drawn Chiefly from Family Papers by His Widow*, vol. 1, London 1868, 594.

∂ OpenAccess. © 2022 the author(s), published by De Gruyter. [CC BY-NC-ND] This work is licensed under the Creative Commons Attribution-NonCommercial-NoDerivatives 4.0 International License.
https://doi.org/10.1515/9783110776232-003

of one of its chief architects: the Prussian diplomat Christian Carl Josias von Bunsen. Bunsen served as Prussia's chief diplomat to the Vatican between 1817–1838, and then to England between 1840–1854. A close reading of Bunsen's correspondence and activities can illuminate the geopolitical, missionary, and ecclesiastical concerns of the institutions and powers that aligned to establish a Protestant Bishopric in Jerusalem. The Bishopric represented an opportunity for the established churches of both Great Britain and Prussia to boost the prestige of their own church by having a center anchored in the Holy Land. It was hoped, therefore, that news of the Bishopric would help galvanize Protestant communities at home, reversing a trend of declining church attendance. At the same time, the project enabled Prussia to assert itself as an equal to other European powers, who had already had various colonial and imperial projects far beyond the European continent. This article argues that the sincere religious beliefs held by some members of the Prussian state apparatus, as well as by influential elites in Switzerland and England, played a significant role in the statecraft and imperial expansion of the major Protestant powers of Europe, even well into the nineteenth century.

Many historians and scholars over the past 180 years have written about the Protestant Bishopric, although in the recent past, only a handful of monographs have been written on this topic.[2] Many of these works focus on the broader issue of British missionaries in Palestine or on the broader forty-year history of the Bishopric in the context of European colonialism. Each scholar has highlighted a handful of motivations or aspects of the Bishopric project. The most recent and useful addition is Nicholas Railton's *No North Sea*. Railton's book studies the creation in 1846 of the Evangelical Alliance (EA), an ecumenical organization founded in London by both English and German church officials, laity, and missionaries, in order to foster biblical knowledge and Christian harmony in society. Railton emphasizes the creation of transnational networks formed by the founders of the EA, which spanned Germany, Switzerland, France, and England, while also including important book chapters on the Jewish connection, and missionaries. Bunsen is featured frequently in Railton's study, and his eighth chapter does examine the Bishopric. Railton's book is an invaluable contribution to the topic of the transnational Anglo-German connections in the middle decades of the nineteenth century. In this article, and for the purposes of addressing the

---

[2] Of these, the most thorough and rich are: Charlotte van der Leest's 2008 unpublished dissertation manuscript: *Conversion and Conflict in Palestine: The Missions of the Church Missionary Society and the Protestant Bishop Samuel Gobat*; Nicholas Railton, *No North Sea: The Anglo-German Evangelical Network in the Middle of the Nineteenth Century*, Leiden 2000; Yaron Perry, *British Mission to the Jews in Nineteenth-century Palestine*, London 2003.

Bishopric, I want to put Bunsen in the center and re-emphasize that he was the crucial figure in the Bishopric project's creation.

Origins

There was an overlapping set of impulses that led to the foundation of the Jerusalem Bishopric. Foremost among them were the pre-millennial eschatological views shared by some British and German elites.[3] For many of these "awakened" premillennialists, the return of Christ was necessarily linked to the "restoration" of the Jewish people to the land of Israel.[4] Although the desire to convert Jews to Christianity was by no means a new phenomenon in the early decades of the nineteenth century, it gained new traction in "awakened", revivalist circles because it was seen as a way to reverse the pattern of decreasing church attendance and religious apathy. Indeed, the waning influence of the church in the early nineteenth century was seen by some as a signal of the impending end of the world.[5] Pursuing this goal, various church and missionary societies in Europe were founded and began organizing efforts to go beyond their own borders to convert Jewish people to Christianity wherever they might be found: from Eastern Europe to the Levant.

With the weakening of the Ottoman Empire after the First Turko-Egyptian War ended in 1833, many European Christians saw an opportunity for a restored Jewish state in the Holy Land. This opportunism included Prussian and English state officials as well. British officials had a combination of humanitarian, imperial, economic, and evangelical impulses that drew their attention to the area.[6] This applied particularly to the UK's Foreign Ministry led by Henry John Temple (1784–1865), otherwise known as Lord Palmerston, who was the Foreign Minister

---

[3] Premillennialism is the belief that Jesus Christ's physical second coming to Earth will usher in the Kingdom of God, a 1000-year period of peace and prosperity.
[4] Restorationism had been a widely held ideology across Protestant Christendom since the Reformation, but had gained significant traction first amongst Pietists in Germany and Puritans in England and America, followed by political elites in the 1820s and 1830s.
[5] See Eitan Bar-Yosef, 'Green and pleasant lands: England and the Holy Land in plebeian millenarian culture, c. 1790–1820', in: Kathleen Wilson (ed.), *A New Imperial History: Culture, Identity, and Modernity in Britain and the Empire, 1660–1840*, Cambridge 2004, 155–175.
[6] The various impulses of Christian Zionism, humanitarian protection of Jews, and economic and colonial interests, as well as the debates among scholars about which of these were most important to scholarly understanding of the Victorian era of missionary colonialism, are quite nicely discussed in: Abigail Green, 'The British Empire and the Jews: An Imperialism of Human Rights?', in: *Past & Present* 199 (2008), 175–205.

throughout most of the 1830s and 1840s and who had worked to open a British Consulate in Jerusalem beginning in the 1830s.[7] Palmerston and other British politicians had imperial and political reasons to expand their influence into the Levant, but their religious impulses were quite significant as well, extending up to Queen Victoria's own pious sympathies for proximity to Jerusalem.[8] By 1840, just as Bunsen had been laying the groundwork for the Bishopric in earnest, Palmerston and the British foreign apparatus had become quite committed to protecting "God's ancient people."[9] By converting Jews to Christianity, Protestants in both countries hoped not only to increase their numbers globally, but also to boost piety at home, and in so doing to usher in the Kingdom of God.

There were also economic incentives for the foundation of the Bishopric as well, as the Anglo-Prussian institution could potentially serve as an important layover destination for tradesmen on the way to India via the overland route to the Red Sea through Egypt. The 1838 Treaty of Balta Liman between the United Kingdom and the Ottoman Empire had also opened Ottoman markets to British merchants and abolished monopolies, much to European gain.[10] Prior to the construction of the Suez Canal in 1869, the overland route was too awkward for the efficient shipment of bulky goods, but it was significantly faster for individuals (officials and messengers of East India Company, for example) than the sea route around the Cape.

Meanwhile, the goal of the new Prussian monarch Friedrich Wilhelm IV was to extend European protection over the Protestants living in Palestine.[11] But matters of statecraft and international prestige clearly also played a role in the Prussian motivation behind the project. By allying with English interests in the region, Prussian officials had hoped to assert Prussia as an equally powerful player on the European political field, while also attempting to diminish French and Austrian influence. Christians made up approximately eight per cent of the

---

[7] Palmerston later would go on to become Prime Minister of the United Kingdom twice during the 1850s and 1860s.

[8] See Isaiah Friedman, 'Lord Palmerston and the Protection of Jews in Palestine 1839–1851', in: *Jewish Social Studies* 30/1 (1968), 23–41.

[9] See Chapter 7 in: Donald M. Lewis, *The Origins of Christian Zionism, Lord Shaftesbury and Evangelical Support for a Jewish Homeland*, Cambridge 2010, 173–210.

[10] For more about the British economic gains and its consequences in the region, see James L. Gelvin, *The Modern Middle East*, Oxford 2005; and Vesile Necla Geyikdağı, *Foreign Investment in the Ottoman Empire: International Trade and Relations 1854–1914*, London 2011, 23.

[11] King Friedrich Wilhelm IV had ascended the throne in June of 1840, and he dispatched Bunsen more or less immediately to England to begin negotiations.

population of Palestine in 1850 (or roughly 27,000 out of 340,000 people).[12] France, through a series of treaties with Ottoman rulers going back to the sixteenth century, had extended its protection over the Catholic subjects of the Ottoman Empire. Russia, similarly, through a treaty with the Ottomans in 1774, extended its protection over Greek Orthodox Christians.[13] Both Roman Catholic and Orthodox Christians in Palestine had established protections from Europe's principal powers, which added a veneer of status and legitimacy to their standing amongst one another. Not wanting to be left behind, Prussia saw an opportunity for their own informal imperial expansion into the Ottoman Empire through an alliance with England, as we will see.

Indeed, by the 1820s and 1830s, Prussia under Friedrich Wilhelm III had already been tentatively lending its protection over Protestants and Germans beyond its territorial borders. But after Friedrich Wilhelm IV took the throne in 1840, Prussian efforts increased significantly. In March of 1841, the Prussian monarch dictated an *Address to European Christendom*, and sent it to the four other principal powers (Britain, France, Austria, and Russia), with the intention of creating a broad European protectorate for the Christians and the "Holy Places" in Palestine.[14] The proposal was rejected by all four powers, most probably because it would have undermined their own respective influence in the region or because it might have unnecessarily complicated the international relationships with one another. As mentioned earlier, France had traditionally been seen as the European protector of Christians living in the Ottoman Empire. Increasing Russian activity in the region beginning in the late eighteenth century had already upset the political balance, while also hardening confessional faultlines. Therefore, the Prussian suggestion to create a pan-European protectorate to replace the existing ad-hoc system was seen as undesirable by the respective powers of Europe (especially the Catholic ones) as a challenge to both their political legitimacy as well as the primacy of their respective confessional majorities at home.

Still, Friedrich Wilhelm IV was undaunted, and summoned Bunsen shortly afterwards to begin his mission to England. The potential of opening a Bishopric by partnering with Britain allowed Friedrich Wilhelm IV and Bunsen to sidestep the potentially more controversial stance of European royal protection for *all* Christians (including those in the Catholic and Orthodox confessions) in the Holy Land, to the narrower goal of only protecting Protestants. As a private,

---

12 Justin McCarthy, *The Population of Palestine: Population History and Statistics of the Late Ottoman Period and the Mandate,* New York 1990, 10, 37.
13 See van der Leest, *Conversion and Conflict,* 33–35.
14 See Bunsen, *Memoir,* vol. 1, 595; and van der Leest, *Conversion and Conflict,* 61–62.

non-denominational Protestant institution, the Bishopric could work to that end while also elevating Prussian prestige amongst its neighbors. Of course, the various British interests mentioned earlier had little to lose by partnering with Prussia on the project. The British royal court likely did not complain that Prussia would be absorbing half of the financial costs related to the foundation and endowment of the Bishopric. In the religious sphere, British missionaries and evangelicals recognized that it was in their interests to tap continental Protestants to aid in their mission, as well.

"Will the Day Break in the East?" – Missionary Motivations

With the political conditions finally right for increased European opportunity in the region, influential Protestants seized upon the chance to expand their own missionary interests. Bunsen, as an appointed Prussian official, served a key role in bringing the plan to the attention of the Prussian king. It was Bunsen's involvement and influence with several leading European missionaries that enabled the plan to move forward. The genesis for his involvement can be traced to a weeklong conference of Protestants in Basel in the summer of 1840. But before we examine that conference, it is first necessary to see how these missionary societies formed, how Bunsen came to be involved with them, before then exploring how they conceived of a Protestant Bishopric in Jerusalem.

In the German-speaking regions of the Continent, missionary societies were also being formed by individuals associated with the *Erweckungsbewegung*. In Basel, a host of revivalist missionary institutions were founded by two pastors: Christian Spittler (1782–1867) and Christian Heinrich Zeller (1779–1860). The *Evangelische Missionsgesellschaft* in Basel (known colloquially as the *Basler Mission*), was founded in 1815 by Spittler to train missionaries to spread the gospel, and to build schools and churches in distant locations: Africa, India, China, and Indonesia, to name just a few. Graduates of the *Basler Mission* typically traveled abroad with English missionary societies, such as the Church Mission Society (CMS) or the London Jewish Society (LJS). Spittler founded a similar pilgrimage missionary society called *Pilgermission St. Chrischona* (known today as Chrischona International), whose first graduates were sent as pilgrims to Jerusalem. In 1820, Zeller, influenced by Spittler and other Pietistic and awakened institutions, founded a *Rettungshaus* and school for poor children in the town of Beuggen, just twenty kilometers east of Basel.[15] The *Basler Missiongesellschaft* and the *Beuggen Rettungshaus* should be seen as contemporaneous with other awakened Christian social-welfare institutions emerging in Germany in the 1820s and 1830s.[16] Such institutions were known as part of Germany's *Rettungshausbewegung*, a movement focused on social reform houses.[17] It was from within these institutions and the social milieu of those who founded and supported them that the impulse to establish Protestant missionary stations in Jerusalem originated in Germany and Switzerland.

Through 1838, Bunsen had been stationed in Rome, and news of his activities there had reached Protestants such as those in Basel. Bunsen had also already been exposed to forms of Protestantism influenced by Pietism, especially from the various embassy chaplains that came through Rome in the 1820s to tend to the spiritual needs of a nascent Protestant congregation there. During his tenure in Rome, Bunsen and his allies came to prioritize worship services that encouraged dramatic adulthood conversion experiences, and which fostered a more emotional type of religious sentiment within the congregation. At the same time, Bunsen was engaged with the day-to-day diplomatic work of negotiations between Prussia and the Vatican leadership. While there were many and various political and diplomatic tensions between Prussia and the Catholic church leadership during the *Vormärz*, the most consequential flashpoint was the issue of interconfessional marriage in Prussia, that is, marriage between Catholics and Protestants.

Tensions had flared in the 1820s after a Catholic priest in Prussia's newly-annexed territories in the Rheinland refused to perform the wedding service without the parents promising beforehand that the children would be raised in the Catholic faith. In some cases, the priest would threaten ex-communication for parents who failed to comply.[18] These complaints reached the Prussian king,

---

15 A "*Rettungshaus*," or "rescue house", was a type of institution grounded in social care, reform, and Christian missionary impulses. Some were akin to reformatory schools, while others were like orphanages. The *Evangelische Kinderheim* at Beuggen was a school designed to educate and care for neglected and abandoned children. See: Freundeskreis Schloss Beuggen e.V., *Schloss Beuggen: Geschichte – Gebäude – Gegenwart*, Lörrach 2008.
16 These institutions served as inspiration for similar projects (such as the founding of a hospital for German-speaking immigrants) undertaken by Bunsen in London in the 1840s.
17 Arnd Götzelmann, 'Die Soziale Frage', in: Gustav Benrath, Martin Sallmann and Ulrich Gäbler (eds.), *Der Pietismus im neunzehnten und zwanzigsten Jahrhundert*, Göttingen 2000, 279–282.
18 Tillmann Bendikowsi posits, however, that these instances may not have all been on account of enlightened attitudes of religious toleration on behalf of those bishops, but rather that some evidence shows that these German Catholic priests may not have even been aware of their own canon laws and regulations. See Tillmann Bendikowski, 'Eine Fackel der Zwietracht: Katholisch-

who stated that such forms of religious pressure (*Religionsdruck*) were illegal and could not be tolerated by the Prussian state. Bunsen was tapped by the Prussian court to lead the ensuing negotiations and diplomatic fallout of the events which came to be known as the Cologne Troubles (*Kölner Wirren*).[19] Ultimately, the episode resulted in several prominent Catholic bishops in Prussia being imprisoned and temporarily led to a breakdown in diplomatic relations between the Vatican and the Prussian royal court. The issue is primarily significant because it was an early instance of a power struggle between church and state (which was primarily Protestant) in nineteenth century Prussia, with both stakeholders nervous that the other side would ultimately earn the loyalty of Catholic people living in Prussia.[20]

Ultimately, Bunsen failed in his diplomatic efforts to smooth things over between both parties, and Bunsen lost the confidence of the Curia and the Vatican leadership and had no choice but to resign his office as Prussian ambassador. But news of Bunsen's actions in this event bolstered his reputation among missionary circles. Following his resignation from the office in Rome in 1838, and before his assignment to England, Bunsen was further immersed in the ideas of Christian restoration and foreign evangelism during a brief period as the Prussian ambassador to the Swiss Confederation.

In July of 1840, Bunsen attended a week-long conference of roughly 250 Protestant missionary leaders, pastors, and laymen in Basel. This meeting naturally included Spittler and Zeller, as they were the founders of the leading Swiss Pietist-based missionary institutions, alongside the head administrator of the *Evangelische Missionsgesellschaft* in Basel, Wilhelm Hoffmann, and the *Antistes* Jakob Burkhardt.[21] The powerful industrialist and philanthropist Daniel LeGrand was

---

protestantische Mischehen im 19. und 20. Jahrhundert', in: Olaf Blaschke (ed.), *Konfessionen im Konflikt: Deutschland zwischen 1800 und 1970: ein zweites konfessionelles Zeitalter*, Göttingen 2002.

19 The most archivally rich and nuanced take on these events that I have found is that of Friedrich Keinemann. See Friedrich Keinemann, *Das kölner Ereignis und die kölner Wirren*, Münster 2015.

20 In the Napoleonic Era, the Catholic church in Germany had lost land, power and resources. But during the restoration period that followed the Congress of Vienna, Catholicism experienced a revival in piety and popular enthusiasm. The Prussian state naturally viewed this with unease, as they had already been assuming increasing control over the church by dictating sermon length and flexing control over ecclesiastical office appointments.

21 The "Antistes" was the highest spiritual office-holder within the Reformed Church in Switzerland, roughly comparable to a bishop. Jakob Burckhardt (1785–1858) was the Antistes for the Basel Canton, and was also the father of the influential cultural historian Jakob Christoph Burckhardt (1818–1897). Antistes Jakob Burckhardt was described by his nephew as "neither

in attendance at the conference, as well. LeGrand was an early advocate of "social Christianity", and used his factory and wealth to promote reform of labor laws, especially the reduction of children's working hours.[22] This diverse group had previously been aware of Bunsen because of his efforts at building the Protestant community in Rome, and they treated him as a celebrity because of these efforts. Bunsen wrote of their reaction to his arrival in Basel:

> We have all long wished to behold you face to face, you have laid a foundation of life for the Gospel Church, which will not perish; our hearts and our prayers have been with you throughout the trials of the latter years [*referring to the bitter fight over the mixed-marriage issue*], and will continue to follow you. May the Lord Bless you in all your undertakings![23]

The significance of this event for Bunsen was quite powerful. For the first time since taking diplomatic office with the Prussian state, Bunsen was being lauded in person by fellow German-speakers and missionaries for his work in spreading Protestantism into non-Protestant territories and for advocating on behalf of Protestantism inside Prussia in the face of what they saw as Catholic aggression. Their support was all the more meaningful, given that he had been forced to resign from Rome after being blamed for the increased political tensions over the mixed-marriage issue by Catholics all across Europe. The entire encounter at the conference struck Bunsen as remarkable, especially as the outwardly pious attendees of the conference would sing and pray together publicly, apparently causing the other Basel townspeople to keep their distance and view them with curiosity, though not with suspicion or animus.

As the conference progressed, Bunsen reflected on the potential ability of this type of religious expression to revive religious sentiments and bolster missionary efforts, Bunsen wrote approvingly of the way that Pietistic practices had become more mainstream by the nineteenth century:

---

a rationalist nor a Pietist", although many accounts suggest that Burckhardt was indeed steeped in awakened Pietism. See Chapter 9 in: Lionel Gossman, *Basel in the Age of Burckhardt: A Study in Unseasonable Ideas*, Chicago 2002.

22 Daniel LeGrand (1783–1859) was a Swiss born paternalistic industrialist who owned a ribbon factory in Fouday, France, near Alsace. LeGrand had an adult conversion experience at the age of 29 after coming into contact with Jean-Frédéric Oberlin (known in German as Johann Friedrich Oberlin), the Alsatian evangelical pastor and spiritual founder of social Christianity in France. LeGrand devoted a lot of resources and energy towards printing and disseminating the Scriptures. See De Felice, 'Daniel LeGrand, The Philanthropist of France', in: Norman Macleod, *The Christian Guest, A Family Magazine for Sunday Reading*, Edinburgh 1859, 508–510.

23 Bunsen, *Memoir*, vol. 1, 572.

> The ancient popular customs of congregational and family worship have been renewed and practiced in the first instance by those called Pietists, which are the Methodists of Germany, as Zinzendorf and Spangenberg answer to England's Wesley and Whitfield; the meetings and societies established by them are gradually discarding the signs of [separatism] and peculiarity, and the movement will gradually subside into general and popular feeling; but as yet is met with a spirit of more freedom outside the German limits.[24]

Bunsen's approving tone of the renewal brought to Christianity by German Moravians and English Methodists is noteworthy, as it was around this time that Bunsen began to appreciate the potential energy for evangelism and missionary work that existed in those awakened communities. Bunsen took note that people were more easily accepting of awakened religion in settings outside of Germany, as it became more mainstream and less separatist than it had been perceived to be in the eighteenth century.[25] Because of the slow acceptance of a less peculiar flavor of awakened Christianity, Bunsen saw an opportunity in harnessing these energies for strengthening the church within Protestant Europe, while also expanding it globally. Indeed, many of the missionaries who went to Jerusalem were first trained in Basel with attendees of the 1840 conference such as Spittler and Zeller.

Bunsen described the events of the conference in a lengthy series of letters to his wife. He delighted in the agenda of the conference, remarking to his wife that "the first day of the festival at Basel is dedicated to Israel."[26] He described how the participants had sung a chorale song, "Will the day break in the East?", in public on the first day of the conference, signaling their shared hopes for new missionary activity in the Holy Land.[27] Having been introduced to the issue of Jewish Restorationism while on a state visit to London in 1838, Bunsen gave a speech on the issue: "The second day, Wednesday, was devoted to the heathen.... The committee of the Jewish Mission met at eight o'clock in the morning... I went in to hear, but after others had spoken, I was asked to speak, and felt that I had

---

[24] Ibid., 574. Bunsen is referring here to influential Pietists Nicolaus Zinzendorf (1700–1760) who founded the Moravian Church (*Herrnhuter Brüdergemeinde*) and his successor, August Gottlieb Spangenberg (1704–1792) who developed early international missions for the German Moravians. It is curious that Bunsen suggested to his wife that the Moravians and Pietists followed Wesley and George Whitfield, when in fact German revivalism (especially Hallensian Pietism under August Hermann Francke) had been a significant inspiration for English Methodism.
[25] Pietism in Germany had been met with suspicion and avarice by both state and church officials in the centuries preceding Bunsen's career. Indeed, state officials had originally passed discriminatory laws forbidden so-called "Conventicles" of Pietists from practicing their worship services at home, which officials worried led to cultish social insularity and theological impurity.
[26] Bunsen, *Memoir*, vol. 1, 574.
[27] Ibid., 574.

no right to keep silent. I told them of Italy, and then of London and McCaul."[28] Bunsen had already been working to make connections within missionary circles in London during a previous visit there in 1838, having given similar speeches at analogous institutions such as the British and Foreign Bible Society (BFBS) and the London Jews Society (LJS). But in Switzerland, Bunsen was able to boast of his English connections to Dr. Alexander McCaul, the Protestant Irish Hebraist who had been sent by the LJS to Poland in 1821 to minister to Polish Jews.[29] By demonstrating his credentials within English missionary circles to the members of this Basel meeting, Bunsen further impressed the leading figures within the Swiss and German institutions who came to support or inspire the mission to Jerusalem. Bunsen continued:

> And [I] could not resist notifying my favorite idea of arranging a Jewish-Christian-Apostolic Synagogue, with school-teaching in Hebrew, or in the language of the country- by means of which, without violence, to work against the Rabbinical Synagogue, and to point out a possible future for the existence of the Jews as a nation.[30]

Bunsen, echoing Martin Luther's controversial words from over 300 years earlier, was convinced that Jews would accept Christ if only they could be shown the superiority of revivalist Protestantism. That he was against the "Rabbinical Synagogue" is rather compelling proof that Bunsen and those in his network were anti-Judaic in their outlook about Jews. Bunsen seemed to hold the pre-1537 view held by Luther that Jews should be treated with kindness and encouraged to convert to Christianity. Although none of Bunsen's views quite rose to the level of violence espoused in Luther's 1543 pamphlet *Von den Juden und ihren Lügen*, it is certainly true that he hoped to weaken and work against organized rabbinical Judaism by any means necessary, in order to more easily convert the local Jewish population to Protestantism. For Bunsen and his allies, the Jewish people were a group that was especially ripe for conversion. It was not necessary for them to become Lutheran, only that they would accept the messianic and divine nature of Christ.

An important influence on Bunsen at the conference came from Gottlieb Wilhelm Hoffman (1771–1846), who had founded the two Pietist congregational set-

---

28 Ibid., 575.
29 Alexander McCaul (1799–1863) was described as "the most influential man of the [London Jews] Society" by Bunsen's wife. See ibid., 601.
30 Ibid., 575.

tlement-towns (*Brüdergemeinde*) of Korntal and Wilhelmsdorf in Württemberg.[31] "We came at once upon my favorite theme, the colonizing by Protestant communities", Bunsen wrote of their first meeting during the conference.[32] Bunsen admired and drew inspiration from Hoffman's work to stem the tide of Pietist emigrants fearing religious persecution in Württemberg by founding the two colonies, and may have offered Hoffman assistance in securing Prussian permission to open a new colony in Posen.[33] Indeed, the colonialist motivations behind this project were just as attractive to these Protestants as any other.

It is useful, then, to think of the Jerusalem Bishopric project, at least as it was conceived by Bunsen in the early stages, as an amalgam. It could serve in its natural function as a church, which in Bunsen's liturgical formulation served as a social model for its surrounding community. At the same time, it was intended to be a colony in the vein of Korntal, or even like the German Pietist model of emigrant-communities of Harmony and Economy in Pennsylvania, and Indiana.[34] It would act as a missionary station, whose millenarian purpose was to convert Jews in Palestine to Protestant Christianity, in order to advance the second coming of Christ. While those earlier colonies' reputations were besmirched by an air of insularity and separatism, the Jerusalem colony would instead be officially sanctioned by church and state officials. For this, the supporters of the plan would need to win royal support:

> [Daniel] LeGrand began by praying that all might be enabled to pray, returned thanks for all for the intelligence just communicated from the Kingdom of God, and asked a blessing upon the people and the Royal House of Prussia – possessors of the Gospel – as Thou hast permitted one King to die in faith, so do Thou conduct the new King in the path of faith.[35]

---

31 Korntal was founded in 1818, purchased by wealthy Pietists and given a royal charter by the Württemberg King in order to stem the tide of Pietist emigrants who were leaving for Russia and the United States in search of better economic conditions, while also protesting proposed "Enlightened" changes to their church liturgy and hymn-books. Wilhelmsdorf was founded as a "sister" colony in 1826.

32 Bunsen, *Memoir*, vol. 1, 573–574.

33 "He brought the intended Statutes with him – we talked them well over, and nothing is wanting to their execution, but – a will from Berlin!", Bunsen wrote. The colony in Poland never materialized. See ibid., 574.

34 The Württemberg Pietist George Rapp (1757–1834) founded three colonies, Harmony, Pennsylvania in Butler County, Pennsylvania in 1804, (New) Harmony in Indiana in 1815, and Economy, in western Pennsylvania in 1825. Interestingly, Robert Owen, the British industrialist who bought Harmony, Indiana from Rapp, was a colleague of the like-minded Christian Swiss industrialist Daniel LeGrand.

35 Bunsen, *Memoir*, vol. 1, 573.

Daniel LeGrand, aware that the previous king had died only weeks before, may have unsubtly included these prayers in praise of Prussia and its new monarch especially so that Bunsen would hear.[36] As the king's representative in Switzerland, Bunsen's presence at the meeting was an opportunity for these missionaries to impress upon him (and hopefully also the Prussian state) the urgency of their agenda. For his part, Bunsen was more than just sympathetic to their shared agenda, as he had been working towards similar aims for more than two decades.

At this conference, Bunsen not only laid the groundwork for a transnational network of missionary organs which would come to support the Jerusalem Bishopric with personnel and funds, but he also was able to act as a mediator between all of the relevant interests. All that remained was for Bunsen to convince his friend, the newly-crowned Prussian king, that this was a worthwhile endeavor. The various people at the Basel Conference (Bunsen, Spittler, Zeller, LeGrand, and the elder and younger Hoffman) had several crucial elements in common despite their disparate backgrounds and careers: an adulthood conversion experience typical of the *Erweckungsbewegung*, and a decidedly latitudinarian, "low church" orientation towards non-sectarian Protestantism, and a desire to evangelize the Gospel abroad.[37] They all had experience in forming and maintaining Protestant communities or institutions: hospitals, orphanages, reform schools, missionary seminars, and even entire city-colonies. Now, for the first time, they had a goal in mind which would direct their energies towards Palestine.

It is important to understand that grand, utopian impulses were what enabled the zeal and commitment which undergirded the Jerusalem Bishopric concept in particular, and evangelical missions in general during the nineteenth century. It is therefore worth examining in some detail the impromptu speech made by Bunsen at the 1840 Basel conference, as it marked a turning point

---

36 The Crown Prince Friedrich Wilhelm became King Friedrich Wilhelm IV on 7 June, 1840, less than one month before the Basel conference took place during the first week of July, 1840.
37 The *Erweckungsbewegung* (awakening movement) in German Protestantism was a mass movement that sought to awaken religious feelings and to cause intense conversions within society, and which had analogous movements in England, the United States, and elsewhere. Sermons, books, and pamphlets spread this movement, especially in the late eighteenth century and into the nineteenth centuries. The movement was especially characterized by a strong emotional response and rousing feelings of sinfulness, joy, fear, and relief. Latitudinarianism as a movement dates back to the seventeenth century, and argues that the focus should be on the moral state of the individual believer, and that it should not matter as much if the believer fully follows or accepts the doctrinaire orthodoxy promulgated by church leadership. In the nineteenth century, this group strove to foster more acceptance of religious dissenters (such as Baptists or Quakers) inside both church and society.

for missionaries as their energies were directed towards Jerusalem. Bunsen claimed that he had not intended to speak at this event, and that he had even wanted his presence there to not be made public.[38] His desire for privacy was likely a political consideration. Bunsen may not have wanted his opponents in the Prussian court, especially during the time of transition after the recent death of Friedrich Wilhelm III, to find out that an important diplomatic figure was directly involved with this group. Hoffman had assured Bunsen that his presence and speech would not be made public, and this gave Bunsen the confidence to address the audience:

> I desired particularly to mark the blessing which had attended the Missionary work in rousing religious feeling among German Protestants, commenting upon the sad condition of whole districts and provinces (to whatsoever Church belonging) from which the spirit of life had fled and showing that only the conception of one universal Church (i.e. assembly of believers animated and united by the same faith and love) could offer a prospect satisfactory to Christian contemplation.[39] [emphasis added]

Bunsen had already been convinced that evangelical missionary work on the Continent and abroad was working to awaken Protestants in Germany. These sorts of sentiments animated Bunsen from the time of his own conversion experience in 1814 at the age of 23 during a visit to Holland and informed his early activities in Rome. His invocation of "one universal Church" is also noteworthy, because although Prussia had unified its Protestant confessions, he was aware that French, Swiss, and South German Protestants were in attendance as well. Moreover, this latitudinarian rhetoric was an appeal to an ideal vision of an ecumenical, pan-Protestant future in which supposedly minor theological differences were overlooked in favor of their common goals. Indeed, the Jerusalem Bishopric, with its syncretic liturgy and blending of both Anglican and Lutheran rites, signified an important step to such a future for Bunsen and his allies.

Bunsen elaborated a desire to shift missionary strategies. Rather than sending a handful of trained missionaries to convert and minister to local populations abroad, he suggested a more coordinated, centralized, and multi-pronged approach. These were the lessons that Bunsen had learned from his years in charge of what was effectively a Protestant mission in Rome:

> As a secondary result I noted the gain in knowledge of humanity in general from the spread of Missions and in particular as to establishing the fact of the unity of the human race. Then further combining means and end into one point of view, I endeavored to show that the

---

38 Bunsen, *Memoir*, vol. 1, 576.
39 Ibid., 577.

work of Missions [...] was but the first step taken for the sake of the second; that what has been accomplished as yet must be looked upon as a proof of the power existing for the renewal of humanity by means of Christianity, and that we are now called upon to found Christian Communities [emphasis Bunsen's], not to aim merely at single conversions by means of single efforts. Every Mission station should contain the germ of an entire Christian congregation, that is to say: the family, the school, the association for accomplishing works of Christian love for the care of the helpless in every way.[40] [emphasis added]

Bunsen's rather utopian description of the potential of centralized mission settlements to both renew humanity and to posit the unity of all races is striking. He believed that the properly awakened Christian community would be more powerful when combined with institutions and associated organs nearby: schools, hospitals, philanthropic associations, and so on. Only in this way, according to Bunsen, could European missionaries achieve lasting impact abroad, with the added benefit of increasing spiritual feelings in their churches at home in Europe. As Bunsen had remarked earlier in his career, "The church needs to be built up again out of the ruins, into which it has fallen through the unbelief of teachers, and the indifference of the people."[41] Once again, we see how the Jerusalem project, in the eyes of Bunsen and his allies, was seen as a vehicle that could directly energize the weakening church in their societies.

The centralization of missionary efforts in Bunsen's conception was crucial. With concerted effort and resources, and equipped with "correct" Christian beliefs, Bunsen suggested that European settlers could win the hearts of the local population in Jerusalem and welcome them into their ideal community:

Instead of multiplying stations, those already existing should be strengthened by absorbing many into one that from each of such centers increased influence might radiate from such as should devote themselves not only to die, but to live and to work the work of the Lord. *The idea of founding such communities by means of converted natives* I dwelt upon most emphatically– as the only efficient means of counteracting the various evils brought upon European settlements commenced in genuine Christianity by the admixture of godless and corrupt outcasts from Europe.[42] [emphasis added]

Bunsen's suggestion to incorporate the "converted native" into the community was meant to strengthen the foundation of future missions, making them more resilient to corruption. This line of thinking was entirely in line with Bunsen's theological and political projects in other areas. As mentioned above, Bun-

---

40 Ibid., 577.
41 Ibid., 160.
42 Ibid., 160.

sen believed that the spiritual activation of the congregation itself was the key to the reinvigoration of churches via liturgical reform. Such an awakening would then unlock the potential of Christianity to unify humanity, in Bunsen's view.

Realizing the Bishopric

Having become convinced of the necessity and viability of the Jerusalem Bishopric plan, Bunsen set to work to influence his friend, the newly-crowned monarch of Prussia.[43] Friedrich Wilhelm IV received a letter from Bunsen less than two months after the Basel conference, in which Bunsen invoked the millenarian trope of the "signs of the times", in reference to the political situation in the Ottoman empire. Bunsen reported in this letter that he had actually *already* written to Lord Ashley and William Gladstone in England, sketching the plan for a new church to be built in Jerusalem. He told the Prussian king that the plan had been warmly and then passed on to the British Foreign Secretary, Lord Palmerston.[44] It is remarkable that Bunsen was already laying the groundwork for transnational cooperation on the Bishopric *before* informing the Prussian monarch about the plan at all. In these letters, Bunsen also made an appeal to the economic opportunities which might accompany the Bishopric, hoping to entice Palmerston and the English Prime Minister Lord Melbourne.[45] Bunsen also knew that the king was taken with the Anglican Church, and sympathetic to awakened Christianity.[46] These sympathies were important in securing royal support for the plan,

---

[43] Of primary importance was Bunsen's friendship with the royal family beginning in 1822 after the Prussian king came to Rome on a tour of Italy, followed by another trip in 1827, this time with his two young sons. Bunsen became fast friends with the elder prince, the future King Friedrich Wilhelm IV, who was only four years younger than Bunsen. Their friendship would last for the rest of their lives and afforded Bunsen significant influence in the royal court. Bunsen impressed the prince with his knowledge of the ancient Church, with his apparently enlightened Christianity, with his love of art and literature and knowledge of the classical world. The Prince came to rely on Bunsen's friendship, even writing to him, "Reading your letters has been a *real* tonic to me." See David E. Barclay, *Frederick William IV and the Prussian Monarchy, 1840–1861*, Oxford 1995, 78.

[44] Bunsen to Friedrich Wilhelm IV on September 17th, 1840. See Bunsen, *Aus seinen Briefen*, vol. 2, 151–152.

[45] GStAPK, Rep. 92, FA Bunsen, A.41, 117–119, cited in: Kurt Schmidt-Clausen, *Vorweggenommene Einheit*, Berlin 1965, 90.

[46] Friedrich Wilhelm IV's religious feelings are well-documented in the historiography, as influenced by the *Erweckungsbewegung*. See Chapter 4, 'Monarchy and Religious Renewal in Prussia, 1840–1850', in: David E. Barclay, *Frederick William IV and the Prussian Monarchy, 1840–1861*, Oxford 1995.

and it is safe to assert that the Bishopric likely would never have happened under the previous monarch.

In the months following his experience at the Basel conference, Bunsen had become thoroughly committed to the project of settlement in Jerusalem. Bunsen was convinced by the necessity to take up the missionary ambitions of leaders like Spittler, Zeller, and LeGrand. But politically, only Bunsen had the necessary influence within the Prussian court to enable the plan. By April of 1841, Bunsen had been called to Berlin and was given instructions on how to negotiate with England to form the Bishopric. Just before going to England as a Prussia's Special Envoy, Bunsen once again visited Basel and wrote of the collective excitement over the developments:

> At Basel I saw many friends; on all sides one felt the spirit of the Mission festival ever active [...] LeGrand [...] awaited me, full of the new idea of Spittler, to settle near Jerusalem a rightly-constituted colony, the kernel of which should be trained at Basel as teachers of religion, practicing self-denial and exercising trades. The center of the thought of all hearts is the Holy Land; and many assured me that with prayer and true affection they look to Frederick William IV.[47]

Spittler's *Basler Mission* hoped to benefit by supplying properly-trained missionaries for the Jerusalem Bishopric, giving his institution and the *Erweckungsbewegung* a symbolic victory and a missionary foothold in the region. Bunsen stood to gain the most. He would be the one to convince the Prussian King of the plan's viability and importance, delivering to the missionaries and millenarians the key support they needed. Bunsen's influence with Friedrich Wilhelm IV was significant; it was reported that before Bunsen arrived to confer with the King about the Jerusalem plan, the King exclaimed: "I hunger and thirst after Bunsen!"[48] Bunsen played a role in his network in which the others looked to and relied on him, strengthening his position with his peers, and ensuring the realization of the Bishopric project.

Bunsen and his allies saw this as an explicitly colonial project, specifically in the lineage of other religiously-motivated colonies like Korntal. Bunsen lobbied vigorously to secure the political support of future Prime Minister William Ewart Gladstone, who during the Jerusalem negotiations was a Member of Parliament in his early thirties. Less than two months after Friedrich Wilhelm IV ascended the throne in 1840, Bunsen wrote to Gladstone:

---

[47] Bunsen to his wife, April 26th, 1841, in: Bunsen, *Memoir*, vol 1, 594.
[48] Ibid., 597.

> It is surely impossible not to see the finger of God in the foundation of an English Church and a congregation of Christian proselytes on the sacred hill of Jerusalem [...] You may now without an effort obtain for Christianity in the Sultan's dominions, not only for liberty and privileges, such as Christian Europe fought for in the middle ages, but even territorial property, indispensable for the maintenance of the first.[49]

Bunsen consistently deployed such millenarian idioms as "the finger of God" with those whom he felt shared his religious sympathies. Bunsen's intention was to appeal to Gladstone's sympathies at both a spiritual level (by invoking the finger of God, and referencing the sacred hill of Jerusalem), and also a material level by suggesting that the joint Anglo-Prussian Bishopric could bloodlessly win territory in the region. This is not necessarily to argue that William Gladstone himself was a millenarian Christian of the most zealous variety, but rather to emphasize more broadly that the people involved in the Bishopric project on both sides of the North Sea were at least sympathetic to those kinds of eschatological idioms.

The Bishopric in Practice

In the space of this article, it would not be possible to sufficiently examine the four-decade scope of missionary activities that happened in and around the Bishopric. Instead, we will focus on the tenure of the second Bishop, nominated by Bunsen in 1846: Samuel Gobat. Bunsen's choice required some caution, as the Anglican Archbishop of Canterbury retained absolute veto power over nominations. As we will see, the selection of Gobat is especially interesting because of his deep connections to Bunsen's network of like-minded Protestants in Central Europe.

Gobat was born in the canton of Bern, Switzerland, to a French-speaking family of Calvinists. In 1818, the nineteen-year-old Gobat had a dramatic conversion experience which he recounted in his autobiography.[50] His conversion experience mirrored those of other "awakened" Christians in the early decades of the nineteenth century: unbelief followed by an epiphany of sinfulness upon reading the Bible, and then agonizing, desperate prayer, and ending finally with spiritual

---

49 Bunsen to Gladstone, 3 August, 1840, in: ibid., 583.
50 Samuel Gobat, *Samuel Gobat, evangelischer Bischof in Jerusalem: Sein Leben und Wirken meist nach seinen eigenen Aufzeichnungen*, Basel 1884, 12–14; and Samuel Gobat, *Samuel Gobat: Bishop of Jerusalem: His Life and Work: A Biographical Sketch*, London 1884, 12–16.

and emotional relief after a solemn promise to dedicate one's life to serving God. Of his experience, Gobat wrote:

> The more I prayed, the deeper became the anguish, the agony of my soul [...] The agony of my soul was so terrible that I filled my mouth with a handkerchief to prevent my crying aloud while pleading for mercy [...] I continued thus praying and crying to God until three o'clock in the morning, when I fancied I saw rays of vivid light coming down [...] and concentrating themselves in an earthen vessel at my right hand [...] On a sudden I felt as if the burden of my sins was taken away, and I experienced unutterable delight.[51]

Gobat's conversion experience convinced him to spend the rest of life attempting to replicate his experience in others. In 1821, Gobat began training as a missionary at the *Basler Missiongesellschaft,* where he too became convinced of the need to convert Jews to Christianity. As with so many other missionaries from Basel, he was sent to England in 1825 to work for the Anglican Church Missionary Society (CMS).[52] Later that year, Gobat was sent on a long mission to Egypt and Abyssinia, spending three years in each country ministering to Christians.[53] The CMS published Gobat's travel journal in 1834, which served as proof for European audiences that Gobat was a skilled missionary and earned him increased attention from Bunsen and the Archbishop of Canterbury.[54] Gobat successfully converted Ethiopian Christians whose Orthodox church had resisted foreign interference for centuries, which further endeared him to both Anglican and German missionaries alike.[55]

The recommendation of Gobat by Bunsen indicated that Prussian priorities for Jerusalem were notably different from those of the English. The previous bishop, Michael Alexander, had been selected on the basis of his status as a Jew who converted to Christianity, highlighting the English desire to convert Jews. For Prussian officials, Gobat's nomination indicated a willingness to convert other *Christians* residing in Jerusalem as well, especially the Orthodox and Coptic

---

51 Gobat, *Samuel Gobat*, 13.
52 Charlotte van der Leest provides a good summary of the natural relationship between the CMS and the Basel Mission. The CMS had more money than people, while Basel had the opposite problem. Additionally, the Basel students were generally more willing to travel great distances than their English counterparts. See Leest, *Conversion and Conflict*, 101–102, and footnotes 10 and 11.
53 This involved preaching to the Christians of Abyssinia and especially distributing a brief edition of the Scriptures translated into Amharic. See Gobat, *Life and Work*, 116.
54 Samuel Gobat, *Journal of a Three Years' Residence in Abyssinia, in Furtherance of the Objects of the Church Missionary Society,* London 1834.
55 Gobat's journal mentions the skepticism of white missionaries held by Abyssinians after they had expelled the Jesuits in the seventeenth centuries.

Christians whose co-confessionalists Gobat had successfully converted in Abyssinia. Gobat's attachment to awakened Christianity further endeared him to Bunsen and also to the Prussian King. In his letter offering the nomination to Gobat, Bunsen wrote:

> You are no more a subject of the King of Prussia than of the Queen of England; your fatherland is neither Prussia nor England: but his Majesty considers you as having, as a tried messenger of the Gospel, a citizenship in the whole Christian world, and [you are] intimately connected with the Church of the Gospel among all German nations by the course of your theological studies, and by *the truly Evangelical spirit* in which you have taught the Word of God and announced the faith in Christ amongst different nations of Africa and of Asia.[56] [emphasis added]

Bunsen was shrewd in his appeal to Gobat's sensibilities as a missionary who, though Swiss-born, was educated in an awakened, revivalist register typical of the Pietistic *Erweckungbewegung* at the Basel Mission. As we saw earlier, Bunsen had visited Basel just six years earlier, to attend the conference hosted by the Swiss missionary leaders like Zeller and Spittler. Gobat's religious sensibilities and missionary zeal were above reproach in Bunsen's eyes, all the more so because he knew that Gobat had married the daughter of the aforementioned Christian Zeller, the founder of the *Evangeslisches Kinderheim* at Bueggen.[57] Gobat was therefore a fitting choice to fulfill Bunsen's grander vision of Protestant institutions stretching from the Mediterranean to the Baltic sea, as he furthered an alliance between awakened religion, social-welfare networks like those operated by Zeller, strictly missionary institutions like the *Basler Missionsgesellschaft*, the CMS and LJS, supported by the principal Protestant powers of Europe, England and Prussia.

The primary missionary aim of the Bishopric changed under Gobat's direction as he expanded the missionary focus to include other Christians. But the tenor of the mission's proselytism changed, as well. Unlike his predecessor, Gobat was not content with nominal conversions, but instead encouraged true "conversion of the heart", such as he had himself experienced, and similar to the conversions related to the *Erweckungsbewegung*. Because many Jews who converted to Christianity lost their jobs and family support, Gobat encouraged

---

[56] Letter from Bunsen to Gobat, March 7th, 1846, in: William Henry Hechler (ed.), *The Jerusalem Bishopric, Documents with Translations chiefly derived from 'Das evangelische Bisthum in Jerusalem' Geschichtliche Darlegung mit Urkunden. Berlin 1842*, London 1883, 131.
[57] Samuel Gobat married Marie Zeller (one of Zeller's eleven children) in 1834 immediately after his return from the two-year missionary journey to Abyssinia.

his converts to take up a trade in order to demonstrate self-sufficiency and dedication to their new faith following dramatic conversion experiences.[58]

Among his other initiatives, Gobat also invited the Church Missionary Society (CMS) to open a mission in Palestine in 1851, specifically inviting missionaries who had also studied at the *Basler Mission* in Switzerland. Although it was not *technically* a part of the Bishopric, the CMS mission enjoyed the personal support and attention of Gobat, effectively blurring the lines between the CMS mission and the Bishopric itself. CMS missionaries were sent to render "assistance" to Orthodox and Roman Catholic Christians who were skeptical of their faith or curious about Protestantism.[59] Although the direct conversion of other Christians was in contradiction of the negotiated rules settled upon by Prussia and England in 1841, Gobat did not seem to care whatsoever. He had also hired converted Catholics, Orthodox Christians, and Jews to act as "Bible readers" to curious visitors from their respective former faiths. He wrote to Bunsen, saying that he felt it was his duty to warn "his brothers, also of other denominations" of their destructive beliefs.[60] This attitude was clearly favorable to Prussia.

Under Gobat, the Bishopric served as a beachhead, enabling and increasing Protestant missionary activities in the region. By the time of Gobat's death, the Bishopric included about 1,200 members across twelve congregations, and had founded 37 schools.[61] The "Bible" schools were founded in close conjunction with the CMS and were staffed by European missionaries. Such schools were an integral component of the evangelization mission implemented by awakened Christians alongside social welfare institutions.[62] The schools were run free of charge to pupils, and were intended to train students to be biblically literate. Missionaries' wives also taught girls in these schools how to become a good

---

58 Gobat, *Leben und Wirken*, 296–297.
59 Abdul Latif Tibawi, *British Interests in Palestine 1800–1901: A Study of Religious and Educational Enterprise*, London 1961, 106.
60 See van der Leest, *Conversion and Conflict*, 112. Gobat also stated that it was not necessary that those in other denominations become Protestant, only that they had a conversion experience and found love for Jesus Christ, as long as they proclaimed that love in their home churches. See Gobat, *Leben und Wirken*, 293–295.
61 *Neueste Nachrichten aus dem Morgenland* 24, 1880 No. 5, 139, cited in: Frank Foerster, *Mission im Heiligen Land: der Jerusalems-Verein zu Berlin, 1852–1945*, Gütersloh 1991, 35–36.
62 These schools must be seen as analogous institutions to the Basler-Mission, the *Rettungshaus* in Beuggen, and even the orphanage schools in Halle founded by August Hermann Francke.

Christian housewife and to run a Christian home.[63] The only book of religious instruction allowed in Gobat's schools was the Bible – no church doctrines were taught. The schools were Gobat's primary method of conversion in the region, and the children were encouraged to spread their newfound biblical knowledge to their parents, as well.

Ultimately, tensions between the German and English churches led to the withdrawal of German participation in the Bishopric in November 1886.[64] The episode offers an interesting opportunity to examine the theological differences between the two churches, especially regarding the issue of Apostolic Succession, or the method by which Christian churches are led by bishops who are ordained and consecrated in a lineage going back to the Apostles. This doctrinal issue was of significant importance to the Anglicans, especially the Oxford Movement. Meanwhile, Lutherans generally had little respect for the sacred nature or lineage of church office-holders, viewing this as one of Roman Catholicism's many corruptions. Bunsen wrote sarcastically about these differences in 1838:

> Now there is not one jot of doctrine in the Church of England which you [Englishmen] do not take from Luther or Calvin, and in which we of the United Evangelical Church [of Prussia] do not agree; if, therefore, there be something which separates us [Germans] as heretics from the true Church; it is the Apostolic Succession – they cannot get out of that argument. Christ died only for the English, for they have the Apostolic Succession in common with Rome and Moscow.[65]

Bunsen's sarcastic quip that Christ died only for the English illustrates one of the few points of Anglicanism that he actually lamented. Indeed, Bunsen disagreed with the position put forward by William Gladstone that Apostolical Succession was "identical with the continued series of Bishops." He went on to complain to an English confidant that "It is the deficiency of the method of handling ideas in this blessed island which makes it so difficult for your writers, political and ecclesiastical, to find the seeds of regeneration in your old blessed institutions, which to preserve you must reconstruct."[66] Bunsen's dismay about what he viewed as Anglican intransigence was representative of the larger Prussian concern about the Bishopric over time. Prussian evangelicals, hoping for renewal of

---

[63] Van der Leest, *Conversion and Conflict*, 191. Van der Leest's entire seventh chapter on the missionary schools contains the best research to date for the impact of these schools on the local communities.
[64] By the 1880s, of course, it was the German Empire which was Britain's partner in this project, not just the Kingdom of Prussia, following the unification of the German nation in 1871.
[65] Bunsen to Thomas Arnold, 13 February, 1837, in: Bunsen, *Memoir*, vol. 1, 428.
[66] Bunsen to John Hill, 26 December, 1838, in: ibid., 493–494.

their church, nevertheless resisted Anglican pressure to ordinate the clergy in Jerusalem as Anglicans.

After the death of Samuel Gobat in 1879, it was once again Britain's turn to nominate a new Bishop. Their choice only lived for two years, and it was once again time for Germany to nominate a Bishop. By the 1880s, however, Germany's foreign policy stance toward England had shifted to a decidedly less friendly tone under Kaiser Wilhelm I and Chancellor Otto von Bismarck. Ascendent national identity across German society made the previous distaste about what German Protestants saw as Anglican supremacy in the Bishopric project become altogether completely unpalatable. Following Germany's withdrawal from the Bishopric, it became a strictly Anglican enterprise, which promptly abandoned missionary work to other Christians and refocused on the Jews of the region.[67]

Conclusion

An examination of this peculiar episode enables us to trace rather profound changes in the religious internationalism practiced by diplomats, missionaries, church officials, politicians, and even monarchs in the 1840s. At its peak, the Bishopric project represented a time of warm state-level relations between Prussia and Great Britain, with cooperation also from Protestant missionaries in Switzerland and elsewhere. Indeed, this essay has shown that it was precisely because of the international, outward-looking religious ambitions of certain types of Protestants in Prussia and England that the two states were able to come closer together for a few decades in the middle of the nineteenth century. In a period otherwise characterized by revolutionary activity and conservative reaction, alongside pushes for national unification, it is remarkable, then, that both states sought to cooperate on such an important project with overlapping political, imperial, and religious implications. By the 1880s, the limits of international religious cooperation were exceeded as the respective states became more conservative and more nationalistic.

While Anti-Catholic animus played some role in the formation of the Protestant Bishopric, the more salient ecclesiastical motivations came from eschatological hopes and evangelical desires on the part of its architects to convert as many people as possible, especially Jews. The experiment allowed Bunsen and his allies to propagate a version of Christianity that was distinctly influenced by the *Erweckungsbewegung* and Pietism, emphasizing the personal conversion experi-

---

[67] Van der Leest, *Conversion and Conflict*, 242.

ence and placing less emphasis on strict orthodoxy. Still, both Prussian and English officials had been anxiously grappling with the status and rights of their Catholic subjects, fearful of potential Catholic loyalty to Rome over their home countries. The Anglo-Prussian Bishopric therefore represented an opportunity for the two principal Protestant powers of Europe to assert themselves boldly and on a global scale, with a reach that had previously only been attempted by the Catholic church. Both confessional and political prerogatives intertwined to realize this opportunity, spurred on by a feeling of competition between nations and churches to assert themselves globally, well beyond their own territorial borders.

German, English, and Swiss missionary institutions and voluntary associations provided manpower, training, funding, and logistical support for the Bishopric, and hopes were high among these missionaries that the Bishopric would serve as a powerful symbol for the spiritual renewal of their home churches. Institutions involved with the Church Missionary Society and London Jews Society in England and the Basler Mission in Switzerland and the *Jerusalem-Verein* in Berlin could boast, in their home congregations and in print, that their work was bearing fruit in Christianity's holiest city. Ultimately, important theological differences rooted in each country's commitment to their respective doctrinal traditions contributed to the dissolution of the Bishopric forty-five years after its consecration, which remains today as solely an Anglican institution in Jerusalem with services in English and Hebrew, showing the limits of Bunsen's network as the religious forces undergirding the Bishopric collided with new forms of hardening, exclusionary nationalism in the 1880s and the changing nature of foreign relations between Great Britain and the German Empire.

If one focuses on the history of Anglo-Prussian relations closer to the end of the nineteenth century (not to mention the bellicosity leading up to the first World War), this period is often characterized as fraught or tense. Despite family ties between the German emperor Wilhelm II and his grandmother, Queen Victoria (whose mother and husband were also German), the state of relations between the two empires between the 1870s and 1910s was cool, at best. Even decades earlier, in the 1850s, England had chafed at Prussia's decision to remain neutral against Russia in the Crimean conflict. These dramatic events unfortunately obscure what was actually an interesting moment in the 1830s and 1840s for the transnational relationship between these two powers. This moment, characterized by a spirit of cooperation and exchange, coincides perfectly with Bunsen's tenure as the Prussian ambassador. The consummate diplomat and politician, Bunsen's warm reputation and deep connections among the English enabled a period of possibility and opportunity. This episode illustrates that

Protestant internationalism was enabled by networks of like-minded people, and sometimes even specific individuals acting alone at the granular level.

The Anglo-Prussian Protestant Bishopric was the product of several overlapping sets of ideologies and impulses. A millenarian desire to usher in the second coming of Christ on Earth on the part of Prussias, Swiss, and British missionaries provided the necessary fervor and passion to pursue such a peculiar and expensive effort, but these ambitions were elevated to the level of state action by only a few individuals, most notably Christian Karl Josias von Bunsen. Their influence at the highest levels of the English and Prussian state and church were necessary to lobby, raise funds, and muster the political will necessary to execute the plan and defend it against detractors. Geopolitical and imperial incentives sufficed to convince even non-evangelical officials within the Prussian and English governments that the plan was worthwhile, especially as it offered the chance to counterbalance the colonial presence of France and Russia in the region. Economic benefits were also expected, and these overlapping material, geopolitical, and spiritual interests led to a concerted alliance between both countries. Still, this episode shows how, even well into the latter-half of the nineteenth century, the degree to which religion and religious beliefs among elites and state officials still played an absolutely central role in international politics, diplomacy, and statecraft.

Sara Müller
Trading and Invading: The Kaiserin-Augusta-River-Expedition and its Collecting Strategies in German New Guinea

Abstract: *This article focuses on a shield from the Göttingen ethnological collection. It was acquired at the Kaiserin-Augusta-River, today's Sepik-River, in the former German colonial territory of German New Guinea. At first glance, it was not acquired during a punitive expedition or by military personnel. Nevertheless, it is worthwhile to take a closer look at the context of the acquisition of the shield. In doing so, it becomes clear that the exact moment of the shield's acquisition can no longer be reconstructed. However, a whole series of aspects become visible in this context. The moment of acquisition casts light on the various people who were part of the Kaiserin-Augusta-River-Expedition, the colonial entanglements of this expedition, and the passing on of information within German institutions. The shield shows the intertwining of ethnological objects and scientific expeditions within German colonialism.*

In 1911, the German doctor and traveller Richard Neuhauss gave a presentation at the Berlin Society for Anthropology, Ethnology and Prehistory. With the help of 212 photographs and several ethnographic objects, Neuhauss talked about his research trip to the German colony of German New Guinea. The audience was especially interested in the objects from the *Kaiserin-Augusta-River*, today's *Sepik-River*. Neuhauss described the Sepik as a "mighty river" with a "cultural centre unique to New Guinea".[1] He criticised, however, that scientific research had "criminally neglected" this part of German New Guinea in the previous years. He concluded:

> It is a debt of honour for the Germans to make up for what they have missed. The ice at the South Pole will still be in the exact same place in a hundred years; in five years, there will perhaps be nothing more to be gained for the field of anthropology on the Augusta River.[2]

---

1 Richard Neuhauss, 'Reise nach Deutsch-Neuguinea', in: *Zeitschrift für Ethnologie* 43/1 (1911), 130–132, here 131.
2 Neuhauss, 'Reise nach Deutsch-Neuguinea', 130–132, here 131.

∂ OpenAccess. © 2022 the author(s), published by De Gruyter. [CC BY-NC-ND] This work is licensed under the Creative Commons Attribution-NonCommercial-NoDerivatives 4.0 International License.
https://doi.org/10.1515/9783110776232-004

The German anthropologist, geologist, and traveller Leonard Schultze-Jena shared this view. He described the situation as "an old debt that can no longer be postponed. Not one of the remotest corners of our African colonies lies that much in the dark [...]".[3] Schutze-Jena had travelled to German New Guinea the previous year. He led the *German-Dutch-Border-Expedition* (1910–1911), which the German and Dutch governments sent out to investigate the region between the German colony German New Guinea and the Dutch colony Dutch New Guinea. During his time in the colony, he also collected ethnographic objects from the Sepik.[4] Based on their experiences, Neuhauss and Schultze-Jena demanded an expedition to research the river and collect its material culture exclusively. The *Kaiserin-Augusta-River-Expedition* met this demand. In 1911 the expedition was sent to the colony. Its central aim was to collect as much material culture as possible from the people that lived along the river. Within eighteen months, the expedition got hold of more than 5,800 ethnographic objects.[5]

This article concentrates on one of the objects from the *Kaiserin-Augusta-River-Expedition*. The shield (Göttinger collection number: Oz 1806) was acquired in Janandai, a village at the Sepik, in September 1912. Objects like the shield, collected during the German colonial period and in a German colony, have become the focus of public and scientific attention. These discussions have centred on how the objects were acquired and whether it involved violence or the extreme disadvantage of one group. Often, this is what provenance research is solely focussing on. By narrowing down the context of the acquisition to the moment of transfer, objects acquired by military personnel or in the context of a punitive expedition receive particular attention. It is assumed that those objects were likely gathered by force. While this often is true, and while these objects should be heavily scrutinised, they should not be the only ones we examine.[6] I argue that

---

3 Leonard Schultze, 'Zur Erforschung des Kaiserin Augusta-Flusses', in: *Zeitschrift der Gesellschaft für Erdkunde zu Berlin* (1911), 494–495, here 494.
4 Leonard Schultze, *Forschungen im Innern der Insel Neuguinea: Bericht des Führers über die wissenschaftlichen Ergebnisse der deutschen Grenzexpedition in das westliche Kaiser-Wilhelmsland 1910*, Berlin 1914.
5 Staatliche Museen zu Berlin, Preußischer Kulturbesitz, Berlin ethnological museum (in the following: SMB-PK, EMB), E 1037/12. The relevant holdings for the expedition were only accessible on microfilm rolls in the Central Archive of the National Museums in Berlin. These are film no. 230, I/IB – South Seas, no. 424, no. 1044. The individual files are sorted with so-called "E-numbers", which are mentioned exclusively in the following.
6 See Gesa Grimme, 'Auseinandersetzung mit einem schwierigen Erbe. Provenienzforschung zu Objekten aus kolonialen Kontexten im Linden-Museum Stuttgart', in: *Tribus/Linden-Museum Stuttgart* 67 (2018), 94–129; Götz Aly, *Das Prachtboot: Wie Deutsche die Kunstschätze der Südsee raubten*, Frankfurt am Main 2021; Silke Olig, *Zeichen am Sepik: Die Neuguinea-Sammlung des*

the question regarding its acquisition is legitimate but not sufficient. Focussing exclusively on particularly brutal appropriation processes drastically limits the scope of research and, thereby, the stories told about collections with colonial backgrounds and colonialism itself. The writer Chimamanda Ngozi Adichie pointed out the danger of those single stories: by talking about people in a single way, that is what they become.[7] I draw on this and Arjun Appadurai's observation that people and objects are not radically distinct categories.[8] Written sources or photographs are often insufficient to clarify acquisition contexts comprehensively. The object chosen for this paper is one example. Its purchase cannot be ascertained. Nevertheless, the very sources that do not allow us to trace its acquisition can instead reveal structures of colonial appropriation and misconduct. Not taking these sources under consideration simply because they do not provide a clear answer would add to the writing of a single story. Therefore, this article looks beyond the acquisition context and uses the shield to shed light on the structures of scientific expeditions and German colonialism in the colony of Papua New Guinea.

The article starts with a short overview of the origin of the shield. Where is it located today, and why does the article focus on this shield? I then examine the involvement of the German and international crew members of the expedition. What was their role in the collection process, and why were they part of it at all? The story of the shield sheds light on another aspect. Since it was collected on a trip to the *April-River,* this article highlights the appropriation of a colony in connection with the acquisition of an object.

Objects from the Sepik

The above-mentioned arguments by Neuhauss and Schultze-Jena were not new. In an endless row of publications, private correspondences and academic journals, contemporary German scientists demanded that German institutions like museums act quickly to collect as much material culture in Oceania as possible.[9]

Seeoffiziers Joseph Hartl von 1912 und 1913 im Staatlichen Museum für Völkerkunde München als semiotischer Untersuchungsgegenstand, München 2006.
7 Chimamanda Ngozi Adichie, 'The Danger of a Single Story' (July 2009), in: *TED Global,* URL: https://www.ted.com/talks/chimamanda_ngozi_adichie_the_danger_of_a_single_story#t-299824 (2021 – 09 – 13).
8 Arjun Appadurai, 'The Thing Itself', in: *Public Culture* 18/1 (2006), 15 – 21, here 15.
9 Glen H. Penny, *Objects of Culture: Ethnology and Ethnographic Museums in Imperial Germany,* Chapel Hill 2002, here 30.

As historian Rebekka Habermas pointed out, these demands and lamentations of the loss of ethnographic objects were ubiquitous in Imperial Germany starting in the 1900s. Collecting these objects and transferring them to Germany led to the emergence of an extensive market for ethnographic objects. Institutions, private collectors and trading firms in Europe and North America demanded more and more objects and were willing to pay increasing sums for ethnographica. The emerging market was aligned with European needs, deepening colonial structures and making violence commonplace in this process. This transfer of millions of objects was one of the most momentous and largest transactions of the colonial era. Scientists like Neuhauss and Schultze-Jena played a significant role in it.[10]

The *Kaiserin-Augusta-River-Expedition* was also part of this transfer and policy. It served the demands of people like Neuhauss and Schultze-Jena, who had wanted an expedition to the Sepik that solely focused on researching the area. The objects collected on this expedition were sent back to the Berlin ethnological museum,[11] accompanied by a list of the objects that also named the location where each object was collected, photographs, travel journals, letters, and reports. In contrast to other collections from Oceania gathered during the German colonial period, the *Kaiserin-Augusta-River-Expedition* is well documented.[12] Most of its objects are still at the Berlin ethnological museum today. However, due to two world wars, neglect, inflation and changing museum politics, several objects were destroyed, sold, or donated to other institutions.[13]

The *Ethnological Collection of the Institute of Social and Cultural Anthropology* at the Georg-August-University in Göttingen is among those institutions that received objects from the expedition. In 1939, 27 years after the shield was collected, the Berlin ethnological museum donated several objects to the university collection. The shield was among 237 objects from Oceania and among seventeen objects from the *Kaiserin-Augusta-River-Expedition*.[14] The donation of the Berlin

---

10 Rebekka Habermas, 'Die Suche nach Ethnographica und die kunstsinnigen Kannibalen der Südsee. Oder: Was die koloniale Nostalgie im Kaiserreich mit der kolonialen Aphasie heute zu tun hat', in: *Historische Zeitschrift* 311 (2020), 351–386, here 353 and 369.
11 Formally known as the Königliches Museum für Völkerkunde.
12 Many thanks to Michaela Hussein-Wiedemann of the Zentralarchiv, Staatliche Museen zu Berlin – Preußischer Kulturbesitz, for her help in locating the relevant files. I would also like to thank the curator of the department of Oceania at the Berlin ethnological museum Dr. Dorothea Deterts for her guidance.
13 Markus Schindlbeck, *Gefunden und verloren: Arthur Speyer, die dreißiger Jahre und die Verluste der Sammlung Südsee des Ethnologischen Museums Berlin*, Berlin 2021.
14 Archive of the Ethnological Collection of the Institute of Social and Cultural Anthropology Göttingen. File Collection receipts 1937–1939.

ethnological museum followed a request from Hans Plischke. He was the institute's director in Göttingen at the time and wanted to expand the ethnographic collection of the university. He aimed to not only fill gaps in the collection but also to obtain more material for teaching.[15] Plischke indeed also lectured about Germany's former colonies at the university.[16] He and many other ethnologists of the time were rooted in the ideas of colonial revisionism. For example, colonial policy issues were discussed during the 1936 meeting of the *Gesellschaft für Völkerkunde*.[17] The idea of using ethnographica for colonial propaganda certainly motivated Berlin's decision to give objects to the university.[18] Looking at the selection of objects that reached Göttingen, the argument that objects from a colonial background were deliberately chosen to become part of the Göttingen collection becomes very plausible. Among the object's collectors are many "big names" of German colonialism, like Neuhauss or Schultze-Jena. The *Kaiserin-Augusta-River-Expedition* was a milestone of German colonialism. It played a critical role in researching the Sepik.

The Shield and the German Crew Members

The description of the shield on the collector's list is unusually vague. Only the month and year of acquisition are listed. The ethnologist Adolf Roesicke was in charge of organising the collected objects. In most cases, he listed them very carefully. A closer look at the list reveals a hand-written addition to the shield:

---

[15] See Katja Gaisenhainer, 'Aus innerer Zustimmung zu den Programmpunkten der NSDAP' – Der Völkerkundler Hans Plischke (1890–1972) und sein Wirken in Göttingen, in: Dirk Schumann (ed.), *Forschen im 'Zeitalter der Extreme': Akademien und andere Forschungseinrichtungen im Nationalsozialismus und nach 1945*, Göttingen 2020, 263–286; Manfred Urban, 'Die Völkerkundliche Sammlung. Eine im Zeitalter der Aufklärung wurzelnde ethnographische Sammlung – ihre Entstehung und weitere Entwicklungen', in: Dietrich Hoffmann and Katharina Maack-Rheinländer (eds.), *'Ganz für das Studium angelegt': Die Museen, Sammlungen und Gärten der Universität Göttingen*, Göttingen 2001, 91–98.
[16] See 'Über die Geschichte und Bedeutung der Kolonie', in: *Georg-August-Universität zu Göttingen: Amtliches Namensverzeichnis. Vorlesungsverzeichnis für das Sommerhalbjahr 1937*, Göttingen 1937, 63; 'Deutsche Kolonialgeschichte', in: *Georg-August-Universität zu Göttingen: Vorlesungsverzeichnis für das Trimester 1941*, Göttingen 1942, here 9.
[17] See Fritz Krause, 'Begrüßungsansprache des Vorsitzenden', in: Gesellschaft für Völkerkunde (ed.): *Tagungsberichte der Gesellschaft für Völkerkunde: Bericht über die II Tagung 1936 in Leipzig*, Leipzig 1927, 1–3.
[18] Schindlbeck, *Gefunden und Verloren*, 98; See Udo Mischek, 'Der Funktionalismus und die nationalsozialistische Kolonialpolitik in Afrika – Günter Wagner und Diedrich Westermann', in: *Paideuma: Mitteilungen zur Kulturkunde* 42 (1996), 141–150.

"Purchase Hollack". This information shows that various members of the expedition crew collected objects for the *Kaiserin-Augusta-River-Expedition*. Not only did different people collect objects along the river, they also had different interests regarding the objects and different strategies in how to acquire objects. Different collecting strategies, people involved, and their roles within the expedition can be revealed by looking at the shield.

Reinhold Hollack was the captain of the *Kolonialgesellschaft*, the ship that was used by the expedition. The *Norddeutsche Lloyd* built it, while the German Colonial Society paid for it.[19] Although Hollack was not a scientific member of the expedition, he collected objects during his time at the Sepik. Roesicke noted in his travel diary that Hollack and his ship crew regularly collected objects.[20] Hollack's position was slightly different from the rest of the European crew members. Roesicke and his colleagues were contractually obliged to deliver the objects they collected to the Berlin ethnological museum. By contrast, captain Reinhold Hollack and his machinist Feodor Fiebig collected objects for their own purposes and sold them for profit.[21] Hollack repeatedly sold objects to or exchanged them with Roesicke. He records in his diary: "At 8 o'clock, Mr Hollack came to give me the places of origin for the ethnographica he had collected".[22] The ethnologist also mentions this proceeding in a letter to August Eichhorn, who worked at the Berlin ethnological museum:

> In practice, it has turned out that all gentlemen who collect ethnographies for themselves first present them to me so that I have the possibility to add a piece to the collection that seems particularly valuable to me. This was determined by the expedition leader, and I agreed with him that such regulations should not be taken pettily and should not be used for the purpose of chicanery.[23]

This statement shows, Hollack was not alone in collecting objects for his own good and passing on objects to be included in Roesicke's collection for the Berlin ethnological museum at the same time. The zoologist Josef Bürgers and geographer Walter Behrmann were also part of the scientific team of the expedition.

---

19 See 'Expedition des Reichs-Kolonialamtes und der Deutschen Kolonialgesellschaft zur Erforschung der Gebiete des Kaiserin-Augusta-Stromes', in: *Deutsche Kolonialzeitung* (1911), 635 and 652.
20 Markus Schindlbeck (ed.), *Unterwegs in der Südsee: Adolf Roesicke und seine Fahrten auf dem Sepik in Neuguinea*, Freitag, 2. August 1912, 156.
21 (SMB-PK, EMB), E 1488/13.
22 Schindlbeck (ed.), *Unterwegs in der Südsee*, Freitag 30. März, 98, Samstag 31. März 1912, 98, Dienstag 18.6.1912, 136.
23 (SMB-PK, EMB), E 1488/13.

They also collected ethnographic objects for themselves and the collection of the expedition.[24] Since Hollack, Bürgers and Behrmann gathered objects on trips to regions the ethnologist was not part of, Roesicke relied on these men as collectors. This practice shows that the collection of objects was not undertaken by a single ethnographer. Roesicke relied on other members of the expedition crew to reach the goals of the Berlin ethnological museum to possess a big collection of objects from the Sepik.

On his list, Roesicke makes it quite clear which objects were collected by other expedition members. Nevertheless, this fact is rarely mentioned in the sources, such as reports and other publications. In the case of Hollack's shield, this information was already missing from the entry book of the Berlin ethnological museum. All the objects collected in this expedition were simply listed under the name *Kaiserin-Augusta-River-Expedition*.[25] Hollack's name is also missing from the inventory card in Göttingen. It remained unknown for more than eighty years that Hollack was its collector.[26] This is quite surprising since it was known in the collection in Berlin that Hollack collected objects for the expedition. One of the rare occasions where Hollack's involvement in the collecting is mentioned is the publication of the anthropologist Heinz Kelm. In the 1960s, Kelm published three volumes about objects from the Sepik at the Berlin ethnological museum. In the first volume, he talks about the unclear origin of several objects that Hollack collected on his trips.[27] The publications by ethnologist Markus Schindlbeck are another exception. Schindlbeck was the former curator of the Oceania department at the Berlin ethnological museum. He wrote extensively about the *Kaiserin-Augusta-River-Expedition* and its objects and mentioned Hollack's involvement in his publications.[28] For some reason, this information never reached Göttingen. One can only assume why this information has not been seen of any interest within the collection so far.

Recognising Hollack as the collector is essential for two reasons. First, Roesicke describes the acquisition strategies of the captain in his travel diary. Although they do not give the actual acquisition context, these descriptions still give an idea of how Hollack acted. He collected a vast amount of objects. Roe-

---

24 (SMB-PK, EMB), E 1037/12.
25 Archive of the Berlin ethnological museum, entry book, VI Ethnographica der Abteilung Südsee 38 152–42 304, Bd. 11, 41 494.
26 Archive of the Ethnological Collection of the Institute of Social and Cultural Anthropology Göttingen. File Collection receipts 1937–1939 and inventory card for OZ 1806.
27 Heinz Kelm, *Kunst vom Sepik*, Bd. I, Berlin 1966, Bemerkung zur Karte und zu den Ortsangaben.
28 Schindlbeck (ed.), *Unterwegs in der Südsee*.

sicke describes the *Kolonialgesellschaft* as filled with objects, and the ship was only cleaned up for an important visit from Privy Council Oswald and the crew of the *Condor* steamer.[29] The cramped state of the ship sparked an ongoing debate between the captain and other members of the expedition, who repeatedly complained about the place being rat-infested. The animals caused damage to the objects, labels, and cords that provided the objects with their numbers which were important to document their provenance.[30] Hollack may have been aware of the value difference between artefacts with and without proper determination. By letting rats destroy the carefully assembled provenance, Hollack may have attempted to level the value between his and Roesicke's artefacts.[31] Furthermore, Roesicke criticised the captain's way of collecting objects: "Hollack entered a small cult house (...) by force (...)."[32] Roesicke saw this as problematic even though we know from his diary that he and other expedition members also entered houses by force.[33] It illustrates, however, that certain strategies were accepted if practised in the name of science or by people who were seen as scientists. These strategies were disapproved of if done with the intent to gain profit only.

Second, the silence of most sources about the shiel's collector is telling. Travel descriptions, letters or articles often conceal the number of participants that took part in an expedition. The myth of the "lonely European", travelling to far-away places, leading an expedition just by him- or herself is a topos in travel accounts and adventure novels.[34] Two of the main sources for the *Kaiserin-Augusta-River-Expedition*, Roesicke's travel diary and Behrmann's novel, perpetuate this idea by putting the scientists at the centre of the story and only giving their account of the situation. When we acknowledge that another expedition member collected the shield, it becomes clear that members of this research expedition were not isolated but part of a group. Collecting a vast number of objects was possible only within a group. Acknowledging that Hollack was the shield's collector sheds light on the structures within the expedition and the situation among the German crew members.

---

29 Schindlbeck (ed.), *Unterwegs in der Südsee*, Dienstag 3. Dezember 1912, 224.
30 (SMB-PK, EMB) E 1100/13, E 1509/13; Marion Melk-Koch, *Auf der Suche nach der menschlichen Gesellschaft: Richard Thurnwald*, Berlin 1989, 174.
31 This quote is taken from Rainer Buschmann's forthcoming book. I am very grateful to him for sharing his manuscript with me.
32 Schindlbeck (ed.), *Unterwegs in der Südsee*, Montag 8.11.1912, 203.
33 Ibid., Donnerstag 3.10.1912, 181, Sonntag 10.11.1912, 205.
34 Carsten Gräbel, *Die Erforschung der Kolonien: Expeditionen und koloniale Wissenskultur deutscher Geographen 1884–1919*, Bielefeld 2015, 217.

The Shield and the International Crew Members

Also, Hollack acted not in isolation while collecting objects. Other crew members become visible in relation to the shield's acquisition. The shield was collected during a trip to the *April-River*, a branch of the Sepik. Trips along the river and into the hinterland were only possible due to the work of local people or other hired workers.[35] "4 Europeans and 45 boys-passengers together with equipment and provisions for 60 days" were part of the trip when the shield was collected.[36] Porters and police soldiers made progressing and collecting possible and supported the execution of the expedition with their work force. Even though their work made the collection of objects possible, their relationship with the European crew members was deeply hierarchical.[37] The oral history memoirs collected by Australian District Officer Laurrie Bragge in the 1970s refer to the *Kaiserin-Augusta-River-Expedition* in several interviews. A resident of the Sepik and the village Yambon remembered Germans at the river in the following way: "My father said the Germans were ok, but their punishment was harsh."[38] The harsh treatment can be read within the travel reports as well. Behrmann reports that the newly recruited porters "were not yet trained and arrived much later than the Europeans. The less than friendly reception helped them to be much more punctual in the following weeks."[39] Corporal punishment was part of everyday life on expeditions in the colonies and in German New Guinea. Europeans did not see porters as fellow crew members but as means of transport. Travel accounts do not give their names but only the number of participating porters. Nevertheless, these figures are the only trace of these porters' existence. For them, the expedition marches were pure exertion. They slipped easily on the soggy ground and had to struggle through swamps, rivers, and up steep climbs. As a result, many of the men fell ill. Illnesses and death were always part of expeditions.[40] For the researchers, however, this was no reason to deviate from their goals. They only took breaks when they themselves fell ill. European travellers could always fall back on a well-stocked pharmacy and recuperative holidays

---

[35] Walter Behrmann, *Im Stromgebiet des Sepik: Eine deutsche Forschungsreise in Neuguinea*, Berlin 1922, 233.
[36] (SMB-PK, EMB) E 370/13.
[37] Behrmann, *Im Stromgebiet des Sepik*, 235.
[38] Bragge Archive, Vol. I Interviews, 0000 02.
[39] Behrmann, *Im Stromgebiet des Sepik*, 236.
[40] Gräbel, *Die Erforschung der Kolonien*, 146.

at mission stations or infirmaries.⁴¹ They also employed porters to carry objects from the hinterland back to the riverbanks and load them onto the ship.

The *Kolonialgesellschaft* ship made a recruiting trip to the coast before the trip to the *April-River* and the acquisition of the shield.⁴² The German colony was in constant need of workers for plantations and police force. The expedition also necessitated a steady supply of soldiers, porters, workers, and translators. The colonial government gave police soldiers to the expedition. They provided security for the European crew members, took on logistical tasks, and led small carrier groups. In addition, their presence was meant to intimidate the local population.⁴³ Hollack's report shows that the ship under his command was involved in the recruitment of workers along the river. Together with governmental and commercial ships, the expedition took part in recruiting people in the colony. The ship *Kolonialgesellschaft* was not only used for collecting practices of the expedition but also supported and developed colonial structures further. The expedition became part of colonial politics in German New Guinea.

Intermediaries and translators constituted another important group. Expedition members were in constant exchange with different people from Malu. This village was located directly opposite the camp of the expedition. Expedition members relied on people from Malu for translations or to get in contact with people in other villages. The inhabitants of the village were regularly persuaded to join the expedition on trips.⁴⁴ On this particular venture to the *April-River*, two men named Gleabob Tuunte and Kambimali Boamni "were persuaded to go along for two months". Roesicke reports furthermore: "Later, when we were eating on the *Kolonialgesellschaft*, the two Malu people left. They had made Baion⁴⁵ understand that they wanted to relieve themselves, had been brought ashore by him and escaped."⁴⁶ This escape raises the question of how these two men were persuaded to join the expedition in the first place – and what made them escape. As already mentioned, several people from Malu were part of various expeditions. According to Roesicke's records, members of the expedition always brought them back to Malu and richly rewarded them for their efforts.⁴⁷

---

41 Gräbel, *Die Erforschung der Kolonien*, 150.
42 (SMB-PK, EMB) E 370/13, 4.
43 Gräbel, *Die Erforschung der Kolonien*, 135.
44 Schindlbeck (ed.), *Unterwegs in der Südsee*, Montag 6.1.1913, 235.
45 Baion is Roesicke's house boy and appears in his travel accounts time and again. Roesicke entrusted him with tasks such as looking after local intermediaries and collecting objects.
46 Schindlbeck (ed.), *Unterwegs in der Südsee*, Sonntag 27.9.1912, 179–180.
47 Ibid., Donnerstag 11.4.1912, 104.

The reports collected by Bragge paint a different picture. Bragge recorded the memory of an informant from Malu named Karandaman. Roesicke – whom the people of Malu called Woskai – nearly took him. Karandaman recalled:

> Woskai picked me up and went towards the boat. My father held me also and cried out. Woskai and Father both pulled at me, and then my father fell to the ground crying with my mother. Woskai said, 'I want to take him to Madang'. [...] My father said [...] 'You cannot take my child!' I stayed in Malu [...] the Germans went away.[48]

Karandaman's account can be read as a case of forced labour recruitment. Young men were of special interest because of their strength. Bragge, anthropologists Ulrike Claas and Paul Roscoe mentioned another situation from Roesicke's travel account. Members of the Kwoma people had killed one of Roesicke's men after he had tried to rape a woman.[49] Violent behaviour appeared to be quite common during this scientific expedition.

Hollack's account of the expedition to the *April-River* clearly shows how many people were part of one undertaking. Local agents were indispensable in penetrating the hinterland. They were also involved in the process of collecting ethnographic objects – by acquiring or carrying them during these forays. As these expedition groups entered villages, the people living there saw themselves confronted with large groups of armed strangers. Their appearance influenced the exchange between expedition members and villagers. Even if objects were not acquired by force, the appearance of the expedition itself already had an influence on the trade of objects on both sides.

As captain of the expedition ship, Hollack was not part of the hikes into the hinterland. His duty was to help with the transport of food, equipment, and expedition members to the areas of research. Hollack also commanded a ship crew that worked for the expedition. Based on his report, the following people were part of the *Kolonialgesellschaft* on the trip during which the shield was acquired: "Two Europeans (Captain and machinist), one Chinese boatman, one Chinese carpenter, four Chinese machinists, one Chinese cook, one Chinese boy and seven natives."[50] The migration of Chinese workers to the German colony to

---

[48] Bragge Archive, Vol. I Interviews, 0000 20. Many thanks to Laurrie Bragge who allowed me to use his interviews for my work. I would also like to thank Dr. Ulrike Claas for allowing me to use her copies of the Bragge interview collection. Due to the Corona pandemic, the borders to Australia were closed and research in the archives was no longer possible.
[49] Laurrie Bragge, Ulrike Claas, Paul Roscoe, 'On the Edge of Empire: Military Brokers in the Sepik "Tribal Zone"', in: *American Ethnologist* 33/1 (2006), 100–113.
[50] (SMB-PK, EMB) E 370/13.

work on plantations and elsewhere explains the large number of Chinese employees in the expedition.⁵¹ It was also related to the changing politics of steamship companies worldwide and in imperial Germany. The advent of steam-powered shipping had changed the way ships worked. The manual skills of the sailors lost their importance, and a common language was no longer necessary for the work onboard. Shipping companies began to replace their crews with Chinese seamen. They were paid up to 50–60 percent less than European workers. In addition to the economic arguments, there were also racial ones. The general perception was that workers from China and other non-European regions could work better in a tropical climate. It was believed that they were better at coping with the heat, which could reach up to 70 degrees Celsius in the engine room.⁵² At the same time, there were also many complaints about the supposed laziness of these workers. In his report to the *Norddeutsche Lloyd*, Hollack complained about the work and bad health of the Chinese crew members on his ship: "The health of the Chinese is still unreliable but has improved somewhat after the selection and strict quinine-prophylaxis."⁵³ The stereotype of the "lazy native" or, in this case, of lazy Chinese crew members was a classic description in colonial literature and reports.⁵⁴ Hollack's description illustrates the ongoing scholarly debate about the health of people that worked for colonial powers like Germany.⁵⁵

There are no hints in the reports by Hollack, Roesicke or Behrmann whether the Chinese crew members of the *Kolonialgesellschaft* were directly involved in the acquisition of objects. Nevertheless, it can be assumed that they were involved indirectly. They were part of the so-called visits to villages along the Sepik. Since Hollack commanded the expedition's main means of transport

---

51 Sebastian Conrad, *Globalisierung und Nation im Deutschen Kaiserreich*, München 2006, 214–221.
52 Ibid., 206–212; See also Sibylle Küttner, *Farbige Seeleute im Kaiserreich: Asiaten und Afrikaner im Dienst der deutschen Handelsmarine*, Erfurt 2000; Ulrike Lindner, 'Indentured Labour in Sub-Saharan Africa (1870–1918): Circulation of Concepts between Imperial Powers', in: Sabine Damir-Geilsdorf et al. (eds), *Bonded Labour: Global and Comparative Perspectives (18th–21st Century)*, Bielefeld 2016, 59–82.
53 (SMB-PK, EMB) E 370/13, no. 4.
54 Andreas Eckert, 'Why all the Fuss about Global Labour History. The New Obscurity', in: Andreas Eckert (ed.), *Global Histories of Work*, Berlin 2016, 3–22, here 16.
55 See Monique Ligtenberg, 'Contagious Connections. Medicine, race, and commerce between Sumatra, New Guinea, and Frankfurt', in: Blaser, Ligtenberg, Selander (ed.), *Transimperial Histories of Knowledge: Networks of Exchange and Collaboration from the Margins of Imperial Europe*, Leipzig 2022.

and acquired objects while doing so, it can be assumed that his crew was at least involved in the storage of his objects.

The Shield and the Appropriation of Space

The scientific expedition not only intensified the intrusion of German colonial power into the Sepik region by navigating the river, entering villages, recruiting people or acquiring objects. The region was also appropriated through the assignment of names. The shield was acquired on a short expedition to the *April-River*. The river was given its name during an earlier excursion to the area. The head of the expedition Artur Stollé, the botanist Carl Ledermann, and Behrmann gave the river its name. Behrmann reports: "We did not want to fall into the old bad habit of giving geographical objects to as many people back home as possible. Mountains and rivers were to be named only after those who had explored New Guinea. (...) So we decided to call the river the April River (...)." [56] In this way, the men used a strategy advocated by another expedition. The *German-Dutch-Border-Expedition* had given the *October-River* its name. Those rivers were named after the month European people had "discovered" them. The same strategy was now applied to the *April-River*. They gave these names in the assumption that the rivers had no name. This practice of naming geographical features shows that European scientists and, by extension, the scientific community did not view the knowledge of the local people about the reality of their homeland as real knowledge.[57] From a European perspective, Europeans were bringing light into the darkness.[58]

Topographical names served to immortalise people or events. By naming the river *April-River*, Behrmann and the other scientists commemorated that it was "discovered" in April. The act of naming was also an act of cultural imposition. By choosing this name, the expedition members were able to create a historical past. It legitimised their colonial presence.[59] On a symbolical level, it also informed other colonial powers that this was a territory of the German Empire. The discovery thus became a seizure.[60]

---

56 Behrmann, *Im Stromgebiet des Sepik*, 133.
57 Bernhard C. Schär, *Tropenliebe: Schweizer Naturforscher und niederländischer Imperialismus in Südostasien um 1900*, Frankfurt am Main 2015, 276.
58 Schultze, 'Zur Erforschung des Kaiserin Augusta-Flusses', 494–495.
59 Fabian, *Im Tropenfieber*, 268.
60 Robert A. Stafford, Scientific Exploration and Empire, in: Andrew Porter (ed.), *The Oxford History of British Empire*, Vol. 3, The Nineteenth Century, Oxford 1999, 295–321, here 315.

Other geographical features such as river bends or rock formations were also given European names. On the journey on which the shield was acquired, Roesicke described, for example, the passing of the Pyramid Camp, which had apparently been named after a particularly prominent rock, as well as the Camel Ridge.[61] Mapping the colony was part of the competition between geographical societies in Europe.[62] New maps were published on a regular basis, driven by imperial expectations and colonial planning. By improving and completing maps, a geographer like Behrmann could make his contribution to the exploration of German New Guinea. Moreover, it was proof of how far the expedition had advanced.[63]

These practices were not as harmless as they seem at first glance. They contributed to generating a discourse in which local individuals did not only dominate the knowledge about the region where they lived. Local knowledge was deliberately denied and erased from history. Geographical knowledge emerged from an outside perspective and as a claim to dominance.[64] Spaces in German New Guinea were explored for the benefit of scholarly societies and the commission that paid for these scientific expeditions. In the case of the *Augusta-River-Expedition*, the Berlin ethnological museum, the German Colonial Society and the Society for the Regional Studies of the German Colonies benefitted from this information. Geographical names given to rivers by the German crew members of the expedition were promoted through maps, international cartographic journals and lists describing the place of origin of an object. In the case discussed here, *April-River* is still the official name and bears witness to German colonialism in the region until today.

---

61 Schindlbeck (ed.), *Unterwegs in der Südsee*, Montag 2.10.1912, 180.
62 Iris Schröder, *Das Wissen von der ganzen Welt: Globale Geographien und räumliche Ordnungen Afrikas und Europas 1790–1870*, Paderborn 2011.
63 Fabian, *Im Tropenfieber*, 271; See also Matthew H. Edney, *Mapping an Empire. The Geographical Construction of British India. 1765–1843*, Chicago 1997; Guntram H. Herb, 'Von der Grenzrevision zur Expansion: Territorialkonzepte in der Weimarer Republik', in: Iris Schröder, Sabine Höhler (ed.), *Welt-Räume: Geschichte, Geographie und Globalisierung seit 1900*, Frankfurt am Main 2005.
64 Kerstin Rüther, 'Räume jenseits von Kolonien und Metropolen: Einführung', in: Rebekka Habermas, Alexandra Przyrembel (eds.), *Von Käfern, Märkten und Menschen: Kolonialismus und Wissen in der Moderne*, Göttingen 2013, 97–114, here 101.

The Shield – Not a Single Story

Returning to my initial question, I wanted to show that focusing solely on the question of whether the acquisition context was brutal or not makes the history of an object a single story. By using the shield as an example, I wanted to look beyond its acquisition context. Based on a variety of source material from different protagonists, it is possible to place its acquisition in a broader context that reveals many different aspects. As part of these aspects, I would like to conclude by mentioning three central moments that have just been presented.

First, I showed that a whole range of different people were involved in the larger appropriation process of the shield. Not only did they come from different regions within the Pacific, but also from Germany and China. Within the expedition, a strict hierarchical order emerged based on the different origins of the participants and the different tasks they carried out as part of the expedition. Discourses about racism, health questions, and the discussions about the so-called labour shortage in the colony influenced this order.

Secondly, the expedition members went beyond simply relying on already established colonial structures. Through their involvement in recruiting people from the Sepik, they actively participated in strengthening colonialism at the Sepik. In addition, they reinforced the colonial presence through unannounced "visits" to villages, labour recruitments, violent behaviour, and giving German names to geographical locations.

Finally, I traced how information related to the appropriation process of the shield disappeared in the files of various institutions. As discussed, it was not known in Göttingen that Captain Hollack was the collector of the shield. This also sheds light on the different interests that ethnological collections in general and objects in particular have received in recent decades and which questions have been of interest to researchers.

This close examination of the shield in Göttingen has shown that it is worth researching objects regardless of presuppositions about forced or unlawful acquisition contexts. Even these rather inconspicuous objects contribute to coming to terms with Germany's colonial history.[65]

---

[65] A big thank you to Charlotte Hoes and Tabea Radtke who enriched the text with their questions and comments.

Tom Menger
Of "Golden Bridges" and "Big Bags": Thinking the Colonial Massacre in British, German and Dutch Manuals of Colonial Warfare, c. 1860–1910

Abstract: *This article makes a case for the transimperial study of the extreme violence of colonial warfare in the fin-de-siècle period. It argues this can be done fruitfully through an analysis of the thought that stood behind such violence. Using British, German and Dutch manuals of colonial warfare as sources, it takes one specific form of colonial violence, the colonial military massacre, as an illustration. Through the reading of a source corpus covering several empires, it is able to show that, though the massacre was always present in colonial wars, the practitioners of such warfare only came to codify it as an indispensable tool by the late nineteenth century. After 1900, the option to leave the opponent an outlet for escape had completely vanished from the manuals of all three empires – underscoring the transimperiality of patterns in colonial warfare and arguing forcefully against any national exceptionalisms when it comes to colonial violence. Finally, the case speaks to the lively circulation of knowledge and mutual observation among empires that also made colonial warfare a transimperial phenomenon.*

In 1913, a Dutch military officer, J.C.A. Bannink, published an extensive, two-part article in a magazine on the Netherlands East Indies, in which he compared the Dutch conquest and "pacification" of Aceh, on the island of Sumatra, with the history of British Burma.[1] The comparison was obviously considered an important one: just half a year before a captain of the colonial Dutch East Indies Army had equally written an article on this comparison for a military journal of the Netherlands Indies.[2] There existed indeed notable similarities between the Dutch and British campaigns. In both cases, colonial forces initially appeared to have conquered the territory by a relatively rapid march on the capital, only to become embroiled in protracted guerrilla wars in the years thereafter. In

---

[1] J.C.A. Bannink, 'De verovering en pacificatie van Atjeh, vergeleken met de geschiedenis van Britsch-Birma', in: *De Indische Gids* 35/I (1913), 145–175, 285–322.
[2] H.L. La Lau, 'Eene vergelijking tusschen de verovering en pacificatie van Burma en van Atjeh', in: *Indisch Militair Tijdschrift* 43/II (1912), 899–909 and 44/I (1913), 23–43.

∂ OpenAccess. © 2022 the author(s), published by De Gruyter. This work is licensed under the Creative Commons Attribution-NonCommercial-NoDerivatives 4.0 International License.
https://doi.org/10.1515/9783110776232-005

Upper Burma (other parts of Burma had already been annexed much earlier by the British), this phase lasted from 1886 to 1895. In Aceh it lasted considerably longer: annexation had been proclaimed there by the Dutch in 1874, but it was only by the time that the two abovementioned officers were publishing their articles that the Dutch had started to believe that the war was largely over.[3]

Bannink used his comparison to draw a number of important lessons about what he characterised as "*Colonial* wars against an *Oriental* people" (emphasis in the original). One lesson he drew concerned the supposed necessity of bloodshed in such wars: "An Oriental people does not give up but before it has sufficiently learned that further resistance is useless: Colonial expeditions without bloodshed cannot generate that impression."[4] Here, in other words, was thinly-veiled advice: colonial wars had to kill, and they had to kill in large numbers. That such wars around 1900 did indeed often kill many is no secret. Images of massacres, frequently showing blithe colonial troops posing next to piles of bodies, are among the most emblematic images of colonial war, associated with events such as the 1893 invasion of Matabeleland (current-day Zimbabwe) by the British South Africa Company or the bloodbaths at Bud Dajo (Philippines, under US colonial rule) in 1906 or Koetö Réh (Kute Rih, in Aceh, Sumatra, Dutch East Indies) in 1904. The above place names already indicate to what extent this violence was a phenomenon that recurred in many empires – something also suggested by Bannink's 1913 comparison.

And yet, historians have rarely written about the colonial massacre from a transimperial perspective, beyond simply juxtaposing different cases and comparing the numbers of those killed. This article argues that that does not suffice and that we should also focus on the thinking that stood behind such occurrences.[5] Why did men such as Bannink had come to believe that massacre was a necessity in colonial war? I pursue this question by looking at knowledge production through manuals of colonial warfare. Even though the term itself was not used, the massacre would find entry into the formation of knowledge on how to conduct colonial war, as will be seen below.

---

[3] For overviews of these wars: Ian F.W. Beckett, 'The Campaign of the Lost Footsteps: The Pacification of Burma, 1885–95', in: *Small Wars & Insurgencies* 30/4–5 (2019), 994–1019; Paul van 't Veer, *De Atjeh-oorlog*, third edition, Amsterdam 1980 [1969].

[4] Bannink, 'De verovering en pacificatie', 43: I, 163.

[5] I make this argument about colonial warfare on a more general level in: Tom Menger, '"Press the thumb onto the eye": Moral Effect, Extreme Violence, and the Transimperial Notions of British, German, and Dutch Colonial Warfare, ca. 1890–1914', in: *Itinerario* 46/1 (2022), 84–108, https://doi.org/10.1017/S0165115321000371.

If we study such thinking from a transimperial perspective, we might also gain new insights. My research indicates that the belief in the necessity of massacre was not only shared across the borders of *fin-de siècle* European empires, but also suggests that this perceived necessity became increasingly prominent after 1900, a development that is historically significant in itself. Taken as a whole, the case is typical, first, for the transimperial context in which the violence of colonial war developed; and, second, for the circulation of knowledge and mutual observation among empires in this field.

Studying empires transimperially is a rather recent phenomenon. The work of Bernhard Schär on imperial science has much advanced the insight that many imperial endeavours and networks were not limited to one particular empire but frequently crossed imperial and linguistic borders.[6] Daniel Hedinger and Nadin Heé have attempted a first definition of the new field in 2018. According to them, two important objectives of transimperial history should be to de-exceptionalise and de-centre individual empires, and to grasp European expansion as a shared project.[7] This is a particularly urgent endeavour in the historiography of colonial violence around 1900. Not only do empirically grounded studies on this subject rarely consider more than one empire in their research design.[8] The field itself also continues replete with theories of national particularity, especially with regard to German and British colonialism. In German historiography, a teleological understanding of the extreme violence of German colonial wars as a pre-history to German "race war" in Eastern Europe and the Holocaust during the Second World War, as put forward by Jürgen Zimmerer and Benjamin Madley among others, has long made such violence appear as a German *Sonderweg*.[9] Isabel

---

[6] Bernhard C. Schär, *Tropenliebe: Schweizer Naturforscher und niederländischer Imperialismus in Südostasien um 1900*, Frankfurt 2015; ibid., 'From Batticaloa Via Basel to Berlin: Transimperial Science in Ceylon and Beyond around 1900', in: *Journal of Imperial and Commonwealth History* 48/2 (2020), 230–262.

[7] Daniel Hedinger and Nadin Heé, 'Transimperial History – Connectivity, Cooperation and Competition', in: *Journal of Modern European History* 16/4 (2018), 429–452, here 430–431, 433.

[8] For some exceptions, see: Ulrike Lindner, '"An Inclination Towards a Policy of Extermination"? – German and British Discourse on Colonial Wars During High Imperialism', in: Felicity Rash and Geraldine Horan (eds.), *The Discourse of British and German Colonialism: Convergence and Competition*, Abingdon, Oxon 2020, 163–181; Helmut Walser Smith, 'The Logic of Colonial Violence: Germany in Southwest Africa (1904–1907) and the United States in the Philippines (1899–1902)', in: Hartmut Lehmann and Hermann Wellenreuther (eds.), *German and American Nationalism: A Comparative Perspective*, Oxford 1999, 205–231.

[9] See, among others: Jürgen Zimmerer, 'Krieg, KZ und Völkermord in Südwestafrika: Der erste deutsche Genozid', in: Jürgen Zimmerer and Joachim Zeller (eds.), *Völkermord in Deutsch-Südwestafrika: Der Kolonialkrieg in Namibia (1904–1908) und die Folgen*, Berlin 2003, 45–63; Jürgen Zimmerer, 'Colonial Genocide and the Holocaust: Towards an Archaeology of the Holocaust', in:

Hull has advanced another thesis of German particularity by interpreting the Herero genocide as the product of a metropolitan "German military culture" which prescriptions proved so ill-suited to colonial war that they spun out of control and eventually ushered into genocide.[10] For the British case, a sort of opposite particularism continues to haunt history-writing: here colonial warfare has regularly been posited as marked by unique restraint.[11] In the words of one of the proponents of this "minimum force" thesis, it had even been characterised by a "general appreciation for the need to avoid bloodshed", in supposed contrast to the approach of other empires.[12]

While many of these assumptions of national particularity have been strongly challenged, explicitly transimperial approaches have not yet taken their place.[13] Here I take one specific development – the increasing tendency in *fin-de-siècle* colonial warfare to insist on the infliction of high losses to the detriment of the option of escape – to demonstrate that it is close resemblance rather than exceptionalism which marks the conduct of colonial warfare by the different European powers in this time period.

A.D. Moses (ed.), *Genocide and Settler Society: Frontier Violence and Stolen Indigenous Children in Australian History*, New York 2004, 49–76; Benjamin Madley, 'From Africa to Auschwitz: How German South West Africa Incubated Ideas and Methods Adopted and Developed by the Nazis in Eastern Europe', in: *European History Quarterly* 35/3 (2005), 429–464.

10 Isabel V. Hull, *Absolute Destruction: Military Culture and the Practices of War in Imperial Germany*, Ithaca, NY 2005.

11 The so-called "minimum force" debate has taken place in two waves, first in the early 1990s, mainly between Thomas Mockaitis and John Newsinger, and second in the late 2000s, with Rod Thornton and Huw Bennett as the main protagonists. For an overview, see: Matthew Hughes, 'Introduction: British Ways of Counter-Insurgency', in: *Small Wars & Insurgencies* 23/4–5 (2012), 580–590.

12 Rod Thornton, 'The British Army and the Origins of Its Minimum Force Philosophy', in: ibid., 15/1 (2004), 83–106, here 86.

13 For some challenges to these assumptions, see: Robert Gerwarth and Stephan Malinowski, 'Hannah Arendt's Ghosts: Reflections on the Disputable Path from Windhoek to Auschwitz', in: *Central European History* 42/2 (2009), 279–300; Susanne Kuß, *German Colonial Wars and the Context of Military Violence*, Cambridge, MA 2017; Caroline Elkins, *Britain's Gulag: The Brutal End of Empire in Kenya*, London 2005; Kim A. Wagner, 'Savage Warfare: Violence and the Rule of Colonial Difference in Early British Counterinsurgency', in: *History Workshop Journal* 85/Spring Issue (2018), 217–237; Michelle Gordon, *Extreme Violence and the 'British Way': Colonial Warfare in Perak, Sierra Leone and Sudan*, London 2020.

Manuals of Colonial Warfare

To demonstrate how the massacre became part of colonial knowledge, this article uses manuals of colonial warfare from the nineteenth and early twentieth century as one of its main sources. So far only the famous British manual by Charles Callwell, *Small Wars* (1896; later editions 1899 and 1906) has received more extensive scholarly attention.[14] Here, I use a broader corpus that not only includes several other British manuals, but similar publications from the German and Dutch Empire as well. Unlike much previous scholarship I do not simply take Callwell's book as a *pars pro toto* for *fin-de-siècle* thinking on colonial warfare.[15] While the work can certainly be considered representative in many aspects, it was also part of a broader genre in which we can detect change over time in several points, even in Callwell himself.

Manuals of colonial warfare were for the most part written by experienced colonial officers, who clearly understood their work as conveying "useful" knowledge to future practitioners of colonial campaigning – the general tenor being that the specifics of colonial war were not being taught to soldiers in the metropole and that only experienced colonial soldiers could provide this knowledge. While the specific logistics, tactics and health considerations of colonial campaigns took up most of the space, most manuals also touched upon the heightened levels of violence that marked war in the colonies. The authors of some of the most important handbooks belonged to the more "learned" branches of the military such as engineering or artillery, to which members the idea of learned publishing probably came more naturally. Decisive however was the perception of a heightened need and demand for knowledge – the publication of manuals therefore was generally linked to phases of increased occurrence of col-

---

14 See among others: Daniel Whittingham, *Charles E. Callwell and the British Way in Warfare*, Cambridge 2020, chapter 2; Daniel Whittingham, 'Warrior-Scholarship in the Age of Colonial Warfare: Charles E. Callwell and Small Wars', in: Andrew Mumford and Bruno C. Reis (eds.), *The Theory and Practice of Irregular Warfare: Warrior-Scholarship in Counter-Insurgency*, London 2014, 18–34; Ian F.W. Beckett, 'Another British Way in Warfare: Charles Callwell and Small Wars', in: Ian F.W. Beckett (ed.), *Victorians at War: New Perspectives*, [London] 2007, 89–102; James Hevia, *The Imperial Security State: British Colonial Knowledge and Empire-Building in Asia*, Cambridge 2012, 215–222.
15 For authors who use Callwell's writing to explore colonial warfare as a whole, see for instance: Hevia, *Imperial Security State*, 215–222; Dieter Langewiesche, *Der gewaltsame Lehrer: Europas Kriege in der Moderne*, Munich 2019, 352–357.

onial campaigning, and thus also displayed distinctive "waves" for each empire.[16]

In the Dutch case, an early wave can already be observed around 1860, clearly responding to the "long decade of expansion" of the Dutch in the East Indies between 1846 and 1862.[17] The first decades of the Aceh War did, surprisingly, not bring forth any instruction literature, even though the war (which had started with the invasion of the sultanate in 1873) turned into the most protracted Dutch colonial war ever. A further manual was only to appear in 1896, when Klaas van der Maaten, a colonial officer posted as instructor at the military school in Kampen in the Netherlands, published his massive two volumes on "East Indies Wars".[18] Coincidentally, this was just before major changes occurred in the Dutch conduct of war in Aceh, changes that would find codification in a number of publications appearing after 1903. Official codification took place in 1913 with the issuance of a new annex to the tactics coursebook for the military academy in Breda.[19]

For the British Empire, the major colonial wars of the 1870s first brought forth a number of essays on the subject of colonial warfare.[20] It was however only the acceleration of imperial conquest in Africa and the unprecedented campaigns at the British Indian North West Frontier in the second half of the 1890s

---

16 For a more extensive chronology of manuals of colonial warfare, see: Tom Menger, *The Colonial Way of War: Extreme Violence in Knowledge and Practice of Colonial Warfare in the British, German and Dutch Colonial Empires, c. 1890–1914*, PhD: University of Cologne 2021.
17 G. Teitler, 'Voorlopers van het VPTL, 1928–1829: Een terugblik', in: *Militaire Spectator* 170/5 (2001), 268–274, here 272–273. On the "long decade of expansion": Jaap de Moor, 'Warmakers in the Archipelago: Dutch Expeditions in Nineteenth Century Indonesia', in: Jaap de Moor and H.L. Wesseling (eds.), *Imperialism and War: Essays on Colonial Wars in Asia and Africa*, Leiden 1989, 50–71, here 55–62.
18 Klaas van der Maaten, *De Indische oorlogen: een boek ten dienste van den jongen officier en het militair onderwijs*, 2 vols., Haarlem 1896.
19 R. de Bruijn, *Handleiding ten gebruike bij het onderwijs in de tactiek aan cadetten bestemd voor den dienst bij het O.-I. Leger*, 2 vols., Breda 1903/1904; R.G. Doorman, *De strategie in Nederlandsch-Indië*, Breda 1913; M.J.E. Bos, *Aanhangsel op het leerboek der tactiek Hoogeboom en Pop: de strijd tegen den Inlandschen Vijand*, Breda 1913. Note that Doorman's book was a reprint of his article series published in a military journal between 1903 and 1905.
20 Colonel Gawler, 'British Troops and Savage Warfare, with Special Reference to the Kafir Wars', in: *Journal of the Royal United Services Institution* 17/74 (1873), 922–939; Samuel White Baker, 'Experience in Savage Warfare', in: *Journal of the Royal United Services Institution* 17/73 (1873), 904–921; R. da Costa Porter, 'Warfare against Uncivilised Races; or, How to Fight Greatly Superior Forces of an Uncivilised and Badly-Armed Enemy (Prize Essay, 1881)', in: *Professional Papers of the Corps of Royal Engineers* 6 (1881), 305–360. The first two texts were originally presentations held at the Royal United Services Institution.

that produced a small wave of book publications: not only the first edition of Charles Callwell's manual, which had semi-official imprimatur, but also several books on colonial war on the Indian subcontinent, and a brief chapter on "savage warfare" in the tactics coursebook of the officers' academy at Sandhurst.[21] After 1900, it was then the rapid British expansion in West Africa that produced a number of publications on "bush warfare".[22]

Finally, in the case of Germany, manuals on colonial campaigning were to appear relatively soon after the onset of formal German colonialism in the 1880s. Initially, it was mostly those Germans who had garnered experience in East Africa who came to share their experience in small booklets. Somewhat later, soldiers who had served in German South West Africa, such as Theodor Leutwein, Curt von François and Kurd Schwabe, would do the same (though the latter also based his work on campaign narratives of several non-German wars).[23] A sort of official codification can be observed in East Africa, which saw the publication of an *Instruction for Field Service in German East Africa* in 1911.[24]

Unlike this last instruction, most manuals were published on private initiative. Consequently, I do not consider them here as expressions of a formalised and institutionalised doctrine in army circles. Neither do I use these sources because I believe they always accurately reflect the reality of colonial war or were essential in shaping thinking on colonial warfare. However, as works that were generally written by practitioners of colonial warfare with fellow (or future) practitioners in mind, they certainly reflect the thought that informed these men and,

---

[21] On the Indian subcontinent for instance: G.J. Younghusband, *Indian Frontier Warfare*, London 1898. H.D. Hutchinson's *The Campaign in Tirah 1897–1898: An Account of the Expedition against the Orakzais and Afridis under General Sir William Lockhart, G.C.B., K.C.S.I.*, London 1898, was technically not a manual but often considered as such. On India, see also the observations of Timothy Robert Moreman, *"Passing It On": The Army in India and the Development of Frontier Warfare, 1849–1947*, PhD: King's College London 1995, 93–96, 120–128. For the chapter in the cadet coursebook: C.M. DeGruyther, *Tactics for Beginners*, London 1899, 268–287.

[22] A.F. Montanaro, *Hints for a Bush Campaign*, London 1901; C. Braithwaite Wallis, *West African Warfare*, London 1906; W.C.G. Heneker, *Bush Warfare*, London 1907.

[23] Hermann von Wissmann, *Afrika: Schilderungen und Rathschläge zur Vorbereitung für den Aufenthalt und den Dienst in den deutschen Schutzgebieten*, Berlin 1895; Carl Peters, *Gefechtweise und Expeditionsführung in Afrika*, Berlin 1892; Georg Maercker, *Unsere Schutztruppe in Ostafrika*, Berlin 1893. Maercker's book, like Hutchinson's mentioned above, was technically not a manual either, but equally consulted as such.

[24] N.a., *Anleitung zum Felddienst in Deutsch-Ostafrika (Entwurf!)*, Daressalam 1911. As indicated in the title, it was however still considered a "draft" at the time of its publication.

as the references to case studies below also demonstrate, such thinking was definitely reflected in practice.

Massacre and Colonial Warfare

In the words of historian Benjamin Madley, the nineteenth century was an age of empire and an age of massacre.[25] Massacres, in his definition, are "largely one-sided intentional killings of five or more non-combatants or relatively poorly armed or disarmed combatants, often by surprise and with little or no quarter."[26] These massacres in the colonial sphere could serve different purposes. They frequently took place in reaction to what Europeans considered "outrages", the destruction of valuable property and/or the alleged killing of European colonists by indigenous peoples. Secondly, they could be also perpetrated with the aim of exterminating a particular group. These two forms were particularly widespread where European settler colonists coveted the land used by the indigenous population but thought the latter's labour largely dispensable, such as was often the case at the American or Australian frontier. Here, as Lyndall Ryan has noted for instance, the two forms frequently overlapped.[27] This article, however, is concerned with a further type of massacre, what Mark Levene has called the "military massacre", but then in its colonial forms. In these cases, an armed encounter generally takes place but the pronounced weapon-technological superiority of one side produces the "largely one-sided intentional killings" of "relatively poorly-armed" combatants that qualify it as a massacre, while the continuing of the killing after the other side has evidently already been defeated (often evident in the cutting down of combatants in flight), corresponds to the typical refusal of quarter.[28] All this translates into the "persistent overkill" typically em-

---

[25] Benjamin Madley, 'Tactics of Nineteenth-Century Colonial Massacre: Tasmania, California, and Beyond', in: Philip Dwyer and Lyndall Ryan (eds.), *Theatres of Violence: Massacre, Mass Killing, and Atrocity Throughout History*, New York 2012, 110–125, here 111. The phrase is Madley's variation on Eric Hobsbawm's famous book title.
[26] Ibid., 112.
[27] Philip Dwyer and Lyndall Ryan, 'Introduction: The Massacre and History', in: Dwyer and Ryan (eds.), *Theatres of Violence*, xi–xxv, here xvi; Ryan, 'Settler Massacres on the Australian Colonial Frontier, 1836–1851', in: ibid., 94–109, here 98, 102.
[28] Compare Levene's characterisation, which however is not limited to the colonial context: Mark Levene, 'Introduction', in: Mark Levene and Penny Roberts (eds.), *The Massacre in History*, New York 1999, 1–38, here 5. Note that Lyndall Ryan understands "military-style massacre" simply as the settler-colonial massacre of the Australian frontier when perpetrated by "officials of law and order": Ryan, 'Settler Massacres', 104.

ployed by imperial powers.[29] In the literature on colonial wars, this is frequently associated with the lethality of new military technology introduced at the end of the nineteenth century, such as the breech-loader and particularly the machine gun.[30] And yet, these massacres were not simply a corollary of the application of new technology – they also happened because colonial armies across empires increasingly aimed for them and thought them indispensable.

Of course, the striving to inflict high casualties on the enemy was not specifically colonial. European military thought in the nineteenth century generally held that the infliction of high casualties on the enemy in as short a time span as possible represented a means of defeating the enemy, both in European and in colonial war.[31] Still, there were important differences between the two. Clausewitz, the great nineteenth-century theoretician of war, stated of European war that "prisoners and captured guns are those things by which the victory principally gains substance;" he added that "the destruction of the enemy by death and wounds appears here merely as a means to an end." Victory, he concluded, "is something beyond mere slaughter."[32] Yet "mere slaughter" was in a way exactly what battles in colonial warfare were to aim for, as is evident from Callwell's passage on the differences in attack in "regular" and in colonial war:

> Let there be no mistake about this – the theory of attack when regular troops are pitted against irregulars, differs fundamentally from the theory of attack designed to meet the case of great operations between armies of the first class. On the European battlefield the end to be attained in attack is, in the ordinary course, to drive the enemy out of his position. (...) But in combat with irregular warriors something more than this is wanted. The mere expulsion of the opponent from ground where he has thought fit to accept battle is of little account; what is wanted is a big casualty list in the hostile ranks (...).[33]

In the British context, this "big casualty list" was often referred to – using a hunting analogy[34] – as a "big bag," as can be seen for instance in a letter

---

29 Levene, 'Introduction', 24.
30 Maria Paula Diogo and Dirk van Laak, *Europeans Globalizing: Mapping, Exploiting, Exchanging*, London 2016, 115–116.
31 See for instance: Großer Generalstab, *Kriegsbrauch im Landkriege*, Berlin 1902, 9; E.K.H. Pluim Mentz, *Zakboekje voor den officier van het Indisch Leger*, vol. II, Weltevreden 1910, 163.
32 Carl von Clausewitz, *On War*, trans. J.J. Graham, vol. I, London 1908, 249–250.
33 C.E. Callwell, *Small Wars: Their Principles and Practice*, third edition, London 1906, 151.
34 That a hunting term was particularly prominent (though not exclusive to) colonial warfare should not surprise us given that European actors in colonial war regularly drew analogies to hunting, see for example: Simon Harrison, *Dark Trophies: Hunting and the Enemy Body in Modern War*, New York 2012.

from a British machine-gunner partaking in the 1904 invasion of Tibet, who wrote home that he "got so sick of the slaughter" that "I ceased to fire, though the General's order was to make as big a bag as possible."[35]

Why were those conducting colonial warfare so preoccupied with killing as many as possible of the enemy? For the military massacre specifically, multiple reasons were in play, not all of which can be discussed here. In part, these reasons were rooted in the specific circumstances frequently prevailing in colonial conflicts. These conflicts often took the form of guerrilla wars, whereby the enemy operated in small groups and employed hit-and-run tactics. This left little opportunity for the colonial army to inflict loss, meaning that whenever such opportunity arose, the practitioners of colonial war felt that the loss inflicted had to be as high as possible.[36]

Just as importantly, however, the emphasis on killing many reflected several modes of racialisation of the enemy. First and foremost, the conviction of European racial superiority made the racial Other appear as inferior and their lives consequently as of little value. A persistent process of dehumanisation generally laid the ground for massacre.[37] This was not a situational process that only took off when war broke out. It was rather a continuous feature in the definition of "the enemy" in colonial warfare as a general entity. This can be seen, for instance, in the stridently denigrating terms used to describe that enemy in the manuals on the subject. "Uncivilised", "lower", or "inferior" races, "savages" (occasionally even more pejoratively "mere savages"), "barbarians", "fanatics", or even "cut-throats" were terms that were employed in these books, evidently without any ironical undertone.[38] The opponents furthermore appeared as par-

---

35 Quoted in: V.G. Kiernan, *Colonial Empires and Armies, 1815–1960*, Phoenix Mill 1998, 160. The term "respectable bag" even appears in the tactics coursebook used at the officer academy at Sandhurst: DeGruyther, *Tactics for Beginners*, 281.

36 As is suggested for instance in: Kurd Schwabe, *Dienst und Kriegsführung in den Kolonien und überseeischen Expeditionen, dargestellt und an Beispielen aus der kolonialen Kriegsgeschichte erläutert*, Berlin 1903, 84–85; Callwell, *Small Wars*, third ed., 106.

37 Dwyer and Ryan, 'Introduction', xviii; Levene, 'Introduction', 24; Madley, 'Tactics of Nineteenth-Century Colonial Massacre', 120.

38 As English nouns, all these words appear in: C.E. Callwell, *Small Wars: Their Principles and Practice*, London 1896, 67, 76, 130, 147, 158, 201; Baker, 'Experience', 904. For a number of other examples, either as nouns or adjectives, as well some Dutch and German equivalents: Heneker, *Bush Warfare*, 162; P.M. la Gordt Dillié, *Bijdrage tot de kennis der oorlogvoering in de Nederlandsche Oost-Indische gewesten*, Semarang 1863, 182; Maaten, *De Indische oorlogen*, I, 11–12; Doorman, *Strategie in Nederlandsch-Indië*, 11; Heinrich Rohne, 'Über die Führung von Kolonialkriegen. Vortrag, gehalten in der Versammlung der Mitarbeiter des Militär-Wochenblattes am 8. Mai 1905', in: *Beiheft zum Militär-Wochenblatt* (1905), 241–256, here 252; N.a., *Anleitung zum Felddienst*, 21.

ticularly treacherous and their violence as wild, cruel and irrational; analogies with wild beasts and tales of torture and mutilation of European soldiers all come up.[39] All this made them appear as inferior, as less human, and their lives ultimately as less valuable than European ones.

A general racial denigration and dehumanisation also translated into an acceptance of substantial *civilian* casualties in colonial massacres, as the lives of groups as a whole had become devoid of value in the perpetrators' minds.[40] Indeed, many massacres counted a high proportion of women and children among the victims (in the settler colonial context, as related above, the extirpation of an entire community was often precisely the point).[41] What is more, because the opponent came to be seen as a mass of irrational savages, the view prevailed that only a particularly harsh blow would suffice to drive home defeat[42] – a conviction that pushed towards massacre, and one that can also be perceived in the quote by Bannink at the beginning of this article. It reflected the emphasis the practitioners of colonial warfare put on "moral effect", their preoccupation with exerting a powerful psychological effect on the opponent through the violence of their warfare.[43]

The massacre has always been part of colonial warfare. The corpus of manuals indicates however that what we have termed here the "colonial military massacre" became even more prominent and found ever more advocates in the years around 1900. In part, this reflected changed circumstances: colonial wars by the turn of the century often had a grander scale than before and increasingly took the form of counter-guerrilla wars, heightening colonial armies' determination to hit out hard when opportunity offered.[44] As the manuals indi-

---

39 For some examples: Maaten, *De Indische oorlogen*, I, 105–121; Schwabe, *Dienst und Kriegsführung*, 5; C.E. Callwell, 'Lessons to Be Learnt from the Campaigns in Which British Forces Have Been Employed since the Year 1865', in: *Journal of the Royal United Services Institution* 31/139 (1887), 357–412, here 390; Bos, *Aanhangsel*, 2–3; Costa Porter, 'Warfare against Uncivilised Races', 342; Peters, *Gefechtweise*, 7–8.
40 Madley, 'Tactics of Nineteenth-Century Colonial Massacre', 113, 116.
41 See particularly the examples from Aceh below. For the analysis of one case with such a high civilian death toll and the consequent colonial strategies of legitimation, see: Michael C. Hawkins, 'Managing a Massacre: Savagery, Civility, and Gender in Moro Province in the Wake of Bud Dajo', in: *Philippine Studies* 59/1 (2011), 83–105.
42 I base myself here in part on private conversation with Kim Wagner, who is writing a book on the Bud Dajo massacre, to be published 2023. See also: Michael Pesek, *Koloniale Herrschaft in Deutsch-Ostafrika: Expeditionen, Militär und Verwaltung seit 1880*, Frankfurt 2005, 195–206.
43 For an analysis of the notion of "moral effect" in the transimperial context of colonial war: Menger, '"Press the Thumb onto the Eye"'; Menger, *The Colonial Way of War*, 164–171.
44 On the change in colonial wars (at least in Africa) around 1900: Bruce Vandervort, *Wars of Imperial Conquest in Africa, 1830–1914*, Bloomington, IN 1998, 185–186.

cate, this changed practitioners' thinking on colonial war not only for these specific cases but in general, making the imperative to kill more central. This is visible overall in a shifting emphasis towards this imperative in the manual literature. For instance, while Van der Maaten's book of 1896 had still shown himself sceptical, writing for instance of the struggle against guerrilla detachments that 'Even if one manages occasionally to inflict heavy losses on such a band, to disperse or even destroy it, new ones will take its place,"[45] the Dutch manuals appearing after 1900 steadily underlined the necessity of "inflicting as much loss as possible;" by 1913, this had come to be put in bold letters in a manual's introduction.[46] In the latter case, the author obviously saw himself vindicated by opinion in other empires: a footnote to this passage reproduced Callwell's dictum that what was wanted was a "big casualty list in the hostile ranks."[47]

More specifically, however, the shifting emphasis is discernible in a turn to specific tactics that were geared towards the production of massacre – by denying the option of flight and by maximising the killing effect of European firearms. As Benjamin Madley has already noted in his article on the tactics of colonial massacre, the as-tight-as-possible encirclement of the opponent proved here one of the central tactical manoeuvres.[48] This indeed became the method advocated by virtually all manuals of colonial war published in these later years, through a curious development in all of these empires: the waning of the so-called "golden bridge".

The "Golden Bridge" and its Demise

The term "golden bridge" was apparently coined by the Roman general Scipio Africanus (c. 236–135 BCE), though it also became associated with one of the great classics of military thinking, Sun Tzu's *The Art of War* (written in China some 2400 years ago), which in its seventh chapter proposed a very similar idea.[49] Both described the precept that when one surrounded the enemy, one

---

45 Maaten, *De Indische oorlogen*, II, 7.
46 Bruijn, *Handleiding*, II, 26; Doorman, *Strategie in Nederlandsch-Indië*, 31; Bos, *Aanhangsel*, 5–6.
47 Bos, *Aanhangsel*, 6, note 1.
48 Madley, 'Tactics of Nineteenth-Century Colonial Massacre', 113–116.
49 Scipio Africanus' words were that "a golden bridge should be made for a flying enemy." Sun Tzu's words have appeared in different translations, but in the 1910 English translation it reads: "When you surround an army, leave an outlet free": Sun Tzu, *On the Art of War: The Oldest Mili-*

should leave him at least one small escape route (the "golden bridge"), as a cornered foe would become desperate and thus especially dangerous. In colonial wars, the notion of the golden bridge gained special relevance and was discussed mainly in relation to attacking enemy strongholds. On the one hand, if an indigenous opponent chose to stay put and defend itself in such a fortification, it offered colonial armies the much-coveted opportunity for a "real" battle and for the infliction of significant loss on the enemy. This seemed to make it imperative to prevent the enemy from fleeing such strongholds prematurely. On the other hand, European soldiers realised that cornering the adversary in such a closed space without any chance of escape would often make him fight ferociously till the end, which could potentially turn into a dangerous and unpredictable situation.

In the nineteenth century, colonial manuals overall seemed to prefer the relative safety of the golden bridge to the opportunity to kill larger numbers of the opponent. The earliest manual of all, Vermeulen Krieger's *Oost-Indische oorlogen*, published in The Netherlands in 1829, advised to attack forts not from all, but only from one or two sides, so that the "rebels" would not be forced to desperately attempt to cut their way out, something which had cost the author himself seven of his soldiers during such an instance in 1820.[50] Up till the turn of the century most manuals, whether Dutch, British or German, tended to agree with this viewpoint, though the infliction of losses already came more prominently to the fore with the advancing nineteenth century. This is noticeable in the Dutch manuals of the 1860s, though these in the end remained committed to leaving the enemy an escape route.[51] Jan van Swieten, the commander of the second Aceh Expedition of 1873–1974, also heeded this principle, leaving the Acehnese a possibility to flee from the royal enclosure (*dalam*), although this was already denounced by his later critics such as G.F.W. Borel, who underlined that such "negligence" was especially grave against a "native enemy".[52]

---

tary Treatise in the World, trans. Lionel Giles, London 1910, 69. On both, see: Paul Pecorino, 'Bridge Burning and Escape Routes', *Public Choice* 184/3 (2020), 399–414.

50 P.F. Vermeulen Krieger, *Oost-Indische oorlogen*, Breda 1829, 68–69.

51 A. Pompe, 'Aanhangsel. Indische taktiek', in: J.J. van Mulken, *Handleiding tot de kennis der krijgskunst, voor de kadetten van alle wapenen*, Breda 1865, 1–116, here 56; Gordt Dillié, *Bijdrage tot de kennis*, 280–281 – the latter clearly paraphrasing Vermeulen Krieger; less clear on the issue is the book by W.A. van Rees, *Handleiding tot de kennis der velddienst en vechtwijze van het Nederlandsch Oost-Indisch Leger tegen inlandsche vijanden*, 's Hertogenbosch 1859.

52 Anthony Reid, *The Contest for North Sumatra: Atjeh, the Netherlands and Britain, 1858–1898*, Kuala Lumpur 1969, 111; G.F.W. Borel, *Onze vestiging in Atjeh: critisch beschreven*, The Hague 1878, 18–19, 23–24.

When Hermann von Wissmann published his German manual in 1895, he reiterated the notion as well, explicitly using the metaphor of "golden bridges" (*goldene Brücken*), which had not figured in the Dutch publications. He understood the concept in a broad sense, not only referring to an escape route from a stronghold but more generally to (diplomatic) ways of avoiding armed conflict. Nevertheless, Wissmann at the same time pointed out that a golden bridge would be wrong if "punishment" was what was asked for, or if the enemy could only be overcome "with the most ruthless means".[53] Equally double-edged was Theodor Leutwein four years later, when he invoked Wissmann's golden bridge as an important aspect of his policy while at the same time arguing that battle should always aim for the infliction of heavy losses and the destruction of the enemy.[54]

This ever-heavier emphasis on not letting the enemy move off unscathed was also evident in the British manuals of the late 1890s. Costa Porter's essay in the early 1880s had still advocated "Fabian tactics" of using artillery and infantry fire to compel the opponent to *leave* his stronghold.[55] By 1899, however, the section on "Savage Warfare" of the official British tactics textbook already proclaimed that the objective must not only be to dislodge the foe from his position, but to "beat him decisively". For this, it advocated an enveloping attack, but still recommended a "loophole of escape for the remnants of the enemy's force", though with the addition that the turning columns should prevent any large bodies from escaping.[56]

Younghusband in the same year equally still advocated leaving "an opening for retreat", while the golden bridge is explicitly mentioned in the first edition of *Small Wars*, in which Callwell spent more than four pages discussing and illustrating the "terrible mistake" of deliberately surrounding certain foes and thus driving them to desperation.[57] That notwithstanding, Callwell too was all in favour of inflicting high losses, at one instance speaking of the "happy dispositions" made at an attack in the Anglo-Manipur war (1891) which exposed the escapees to "loss so serious as almost to annihilate them."[58] Interestingly, Callwell limited the golden bridge to small wars, informed by his conviction that "sav-

---

53 Wissmann, *Afrika*, 17–18.
54 Theodor Leutwein, *Die Kämpfe der kaiserlichen Schutztruppe in Deutsch-Südwestafrika in den Jahren 1894–1896, sowie die sich hieraus für uns ergebenden Lehren: Vortrag, gehalten in der Militärischen Gesellschaft zu Berlin am 19. Februar 1898*, Berlin 1899, 5.
55 Costa Porter, 'Warfare against Uncivilised Races', 339–340.
56 DeGruyther, *Tactics for Beginners*, 273–274.
57 Younghusband, *Indian Frontier Warfare*, 39; Callwell, *Small Wars*, 88–92.
58 Callwell, *Small Wars*, 91.

ages" and the like "give no quarter and expect none" and would therefore fight desperately when hemmed in, instead of surrendering.⁵⁹

As the above makes abundantly clear, the adherence by the practitioners of colonial warfare to the idea of the golden bridge in the nineteenth century had little to do with a desire to limit enemy casualties and much more with concerns about one's own safety. Probably, the demise of the idea after 1900 therefore also had a lot to do with the general increase in confidence and dwindling caution among colonial soldiers, conditioned by the perceived inexorable advance of colonial conquest over the preceding decades.⁶⁰ Nevertheless, the demise also shows a growing obsession with the infliction of losses.

As stated before, this shift after the turn of the century also reflected changes on the ground. At least in the Aceh War, such changes are detectable in some of the sources. For instance, the lieutenant De Josselin de Jong of the East Indies army wrote in a letter (1897) about the occupation of a nearly impregnable Acehnese stronghold which had been deserted by the defenders. While the lieutenant's company was celebrating this as a success, they were indignant to hear the chief of staff grumbling that the success was very nice, but that he would have found it even nicer if the fastness had been taken by fighting, so that many Acehnese would have perished in the endeavour.⁶¹ Success certainly came to be identified with a large number of dead remaining behind in the Acehnese *bentengs* (forts): one year later another soldier reported 71 dead bodies left behind in two taken fortifications, a sight which he interpreted as a "brilliant success" and "certainly [*wel*] a proof of their complete defeat."⁶²

Little wonder, then, that such views slowly also found their way into Dutch manuals. The 1903 volume by De Bruijn still cautioned that completely surrounding the enemy would generally cost the attackers many casualties, but did not explicitly discourage such a proceeding anymore.⁶³ Doorman around the same time already betrayed a stronger change in attitude by stating that if the opportunity offered itself to inflict heavy losses on the opponent, commanders should not shrink from "heavy sacrifices" amongst their own ranks.⁶⁴ The shift was most explicitly codified in 1913, when Bos published his handbook. The author insisted that no serious losses could be inflicted on an enemy who fled his stronghold,

---

59 Ibid., 88.
60 On this development, see also: Menger, *The Colonial Way of War*, 175–177.
61 Letter J. Ph. de Josselin de Jong to his brother Gerard 23 October 1897, Nederlands Instituut voor Militaire Historie, The Hague (NIMH), t. 57, inv. nr. 6415, 3.
62 D.E. Gerritsen, Dagboek [diary], NIMH, t. 543, inv. nr. 72, f. 100.
63 Bruijn, *Handleiding*, I, 46–47.
64 Doorman, *Strategie in Nederlandsch-Indië*, 31.

and therefore declared that the only solution for this was the use of so-called *afsluitingstroepen* ("closing-off troops") who would cut off all escape routes.[65] The fact that a new word had developed for such special duty troops signals how the practice had become institutionalised, and indeed we find multiple mentions of the practice (though not the specific term yet) in the infamous massacres perpetrated by the Van Daalen expedition of 1904 in Gayo- and Alasland.[66] It was certainly also telling that Bos' manual dared reject the heroic immediate frontal storming of strongholds, given all the sentimental value attached to it in the military at the time.[67] Though he still deemed such action "beautiful", he still dismissed it as it would thwart the desired body count.[68]

The focus above has been on the Dutch case, where the shift can be traced in particular detail in written material. For the British and German cases, the manuals do not allow such a detailed reconstruction. Nevertheless, what is clear is that references to leaving an escape route simply vanished after the turn of the century. Callwell in the third edition of *Small Wars* (1906) chose to omit *entirely* the section on the golden bridge that had occupied more than four pages in his first and second edition.[69] Other British manuals published after 1900 were also silent on the principle. In German post-1900 handbooks, the issue is somewhat sparsely treated, but when Curt von François in 1900 spoke of surrounding strongholds in German South West Africa he declared that the adversary should only realise his encirclement when it was too late to escape, and that after completion of the encirclement rifle and artillery fire would have to aim for "every target that offers itself".[70] Two years later, Kurd Schwabe quoted these passages from Von François. He equally held that "The opponent must be invested tightly and from all sides", and saw no reason not to do so despite his acknowledgement of the fierce resistance that such procedure provoked.[71]

As a last remark on the German case, it should be noted that the 1911 manual for field service in German East Africa is the only one of all early twentieth-century manuals surveyed here which actually still included a mention of a "possi-

---

65 Bos, *Aanhangsel*, 47.
66 See, among others: J.C.J. Kempees, *De tocht van Overste Van Daalen door de Gajo-, Alas- en Bataklanden: 8 februari tot 23 juli 1904*, Amsterdam 1905, 64–65, 168, 230.
67 The heroic final (bayonet) charge held a special place in the Western military imagination at the time: John Ellis, *The Social History of the Machine Gun*, Baltimore 1986 [1975], 17–18.
68 Bos, *Aanhangsel*, 134–135.
69 Compare chapter IX of the first edition and the corresponding chapter VIII in the 1906 edition.
70 Curt von François, *Kriegführung in Süd-Afrika*, Berlin 1900, 31, 45–46.
71 Schwabe, *Dienst und Kriegführung*, 90, 102–103.

bility of escape" (*Möglichkeit eines Entweichens*) for the enemy.⁷² Not too much significance should be attached to this, though. First, the publication did also perceive attacks on strongholds as favourable opportunities to deal "a forceful blow", and secondly, it affirmed that the terrain over which the opponent could potentially flee should be covered by machine gun fire – the outcome in that case would probably only have differed little from that of complete encirclement.⁷³ Nevertheless, it set the publication apart from other contemporary ones, which had chosen to omit this precept completely.

Conclusion

What the blithe language of "golden bridges" and the euphemistic formulations of military manuals concealed, was what the increasing tendency to deny the opponent an escape route meant to those who became the victim of the growing colonial obsession with inflicting high losses. Hemmed in in (natural) strongholds with nowhere to go or with their flight routes covered by fire, Africans or Asians were often mercilessly shot down by the hundreds. In Natal in 1906, for instance, colonial troops surrounded Zulu fighters at Mome Gorge who had risen under *inkosi* Bhambatha, and showed no mercy. Making use of dumdum bullets, machine guns and field guns, they killed 575 while losing only three men themselves; Zulu deaths could even have been far higher had not the drive been halted early by a mistaken order to assemble.⁷⁴ Approximately one month later, the procedure was repeated at Izinsimba, where 543 men were massacred after being surrounded by the colonial militia who it seems had orders to take no prisoners.⁷⁵

Similarly, in the Gayo and Alas lands in Aceh, Dutch commanders used "closing-off troops" to cover the escape routes of the fortified villages of the locals, then stormed the ramparts and shot down virtually everyone inside. The ac-

---

72 N.a., *Anleitung zum Felddienst*, 134.
73 Ibid., 129, 134.
74 Jeff Guy, *Remembering the Rebellion: The Zulu Uprising of 1906*, Scottsville 2006, 85–86, 120–123; Ellis, *Social History of the Machine Gun*, 101; K.G. Gillings, 'The Bambata Rebellion of 1906: Nkandla Operations and the Battle of Mome Gorge 10 June 1906', in: *Krygshistoriese Tydskrif/Military History Journal* 8/1 (1989), 21–31. Ulrike Lindner has also discussed this war in her entangled history of British and German colonialism in Africa, see: Ulrike Lindner, *Koloniale Begegnungen: Deutschland und Großbritannien als Imperialmächte in Afrika 1880–1914*, Frankfurt 2011, 281–293.
75 Guy, *Remembering the Rebellion*, 162–164.

ceptance of also killing large numbers of women and children is evident in these attacks; at Koetö Réh, the site of the worst massacre, 561 humans were killed, of which 189 were women and 59 children. The urge to kill as many men as possible trumped the will to save women and children; a Dutch narrative of the attack on Badaq related for instance how fleeing women and children had been pursued by volley fire after men with rifles had started joining the former's flight.[76] Significantly, one year later a *British* guide for military officers on the subject of the Netherlands East Indies defended the Dutch actions, writing that the killing of "some hundred" Acehnese women and children "naturally drew much angry comment from the European press, but it is not certain that much blame attaches to the Dutch troops, for it is the practice of the natives to fight from the protection of their huts, which are frequently crowded with non-combatants."[77]

If these events have a clear sense of overkill to them, it is precisely because overkill was increasingly what practitioners of colonial warfare aimed for. The death toll had to be exceptionally high; by 1900, an escape of a large body of the enemy was not considered acceptable anymore. In the cynical language of the perpetrators, the "golden bridge" was substituted for by the "big bag". If on the ground there apparently was a certain decrease in colonial bloodshed after the first years of the twentieth century, as has been claimed, it was thus definitely not because thinking on colonial warfare had grown more benevolent.[78] Rather, as John Ellis noted, most resistance had already been bloodily crushed in the years before, in part precisely by such massacres as were now openly being recommended in manuals of colonial warfare.[79]

Importantly, all this was a transimperial development. Colonial warfare did never develop in national isolation. A perusal of the manuals clearly demonstrates there was no purported "general appreciation for the need to avoid bloodshed" in British thinking on colonial warfare; rather Callwell's "big casualty list" was the norm. Neither thus was such large-scale killing the product of a supposedly specifically German disposition. Actually, early German manuals were

---

76 Paul Bijl, *Emerging Memory: Photographs of Colonial Atrocity in Dutch Cultural Remembrance*, Amsterdam 2015, 45–50; Veer, *Atjeh-oorlog*, 267–272; Kempees, *Tocht van Overste Van Daalen*, 66, 230.
77 Military report on the Netherlands' possessions in the East Indies. Prepared in the General Staff, War Office. 1905. The National Archives Kew, WO 33/359, 21.
78 Several historians have remarked on the burst of colonial bloodshed after 1900, followed by a relative decrease in bloodletting, see for instance: Ellis, *Social History of the Machine Gun*, 100; Dirk van Laak, 'Koloniale (Un-)Ordnung. Kolonien als "Laboratorien der Moderne"?', in: Sebastian Conrad and Jürgen Osterhammel (eds.), *Das Kaiserreich transnational: Deutschland in der Welt 1871–1914*, Göttingen 2004, 257–279, here 261.
79 Ellis, *Social History of the Machine Gun*, 100.

rather subdued on this supposed necessity to kill; they seemed to still rely more on the alleged "moral effect" of audacious attacks.[80] Thus, a peculiarly German destructiveness born of a specific "military culture" cannot be observed at the beginning. When Germans later came to speak of the necessity to invest the enemy in its stronghold in order to deal a "firm blow", this was apparently a "lesson" they had learned in colonial warfare. It is worth keeping this in mind given that Isabel Hull in particular has portrayed the botched German attempt at encirclement in the battle of Waterberg (German-Herero War) as important proof of a supposed dogmatic clinging to a German military culture wholly unsuitable for colonial warfare, which finally was to explain the descent into genocide.[81] It should give us pause when the 1913 Dutch manual by Bos urged "complete encirclement" of enemy positions, quoting, without further comment, a passage from Schwabe's *German* colonial handbook of 1903 to support this point.[82] Obviously, Bos did not perceive something particularly German there, but instead a common understanding of the "necessities" of colonial warfare.

The story of the waning "golden bridge" and the consequent increasing lethality of colonial warfare around 1900 thus shows us how a transimperial reading can advance our understanding of the phenomenon of colonial warfare. To place this phenomenon more frequently and more systematically in its transimperial context remains an urgent task. If contemporaries like Bannink, quoted at beginning of this article, frequently considered cases from different empires *together* in an attempt to further understanding, why should not we historians?

---

80 Curt Morgen believed that against a rapidly advancing enemy, the moral effect of a last-minute counter-sally would be more effective than any losses inflicted through rifle fire, however extensive those losses were: C. Morgen, *Kriegs- und Expeditionsführung in Afrika*, Berlin 1893, 38. See also: Peters, *Gefechtweise*, 13. This early manual, like Wissmann's, does not explicitly discuss the necessity of inflicting high losses.
81 This is repeatedly stressed by Isabel Hull, see among others: Hull, *Absolute Destruction*, 3, 33–34, 42, 45.
82 Bos, *Aanhangsel*, 140.

Riley Linebaugh
Protecting Bad Intel in a Dirty War: Britain's Emergency in Kenya and the Origins of 'Migrated Archives', 1952–1960

Abstract: *This chapter analyzes the colonial recordkeeping practices established in Kenya during the Emergency (1952–1960) through the reorganization of intelligence services. In doing so, it analyzes information management during the Emergency as an attempt to establish and control one legitimate perspective of the counter-insurgency. The British Colonial Government (BCG) responded to its operational ignorance during the Emergency with a violent system of screening, a flimsy use of legal evidence, a program of censorship and propaganda and lastly a system of securitizing documents. The latter would form the basis of the regulation of Kenya's archives, which the administration gestured to only in its final years in power. Thus, the process of record removal at the end of colonial rule was according to a similar logic as in the documents' creation: to secure intelligence and conceal the role of both the BCG and Colonial Office in the systematic use of violence.*

"There are some people, be they black or white, who don't want others to rise above them. They want to be the source of all knowledge and share it piecemeal to others less endowed."
– Ngũgĩ wa Thiong'o, 1964.[1]

"The arrangement, security and access to Government classified papers are matters for the Government, and fall within the confines of official secrecy." – Tom Neil, 1960.[2]

"We know that certain people have realized the possibilities and advantages of penetrating the Government's secrets. This is a threat to security which is bound to increase, and

---

Note: This chapter is based on the author's dissertation, "Curating the Colonial Past: Britain's 'Migrated Archives' and the Struggle for Kenya's History", and a version of it was discussed at the 2019 workshop, "European History across Boundaries", a cooperation between the University of Oxford and the Leibniz Institute of European History.

1 Ngũgĩ wa Thiong'o, *Weep Not, Child*, Oxford 1987, 21. Ngũgĩ wa Thiong'o is a Kenyan writer who is well known for his linguistic advocacy of Kikuyu and other non-European languages. His debut novel, here cited, focuses on the relationship between Africans and white settlers in colonial Kenya.
2 TNA, FCO 141/6540, File Note Ref. 79–80, T. Neil, 24 October 1960.

 OpenAccess. © 2022 the author(s), published by De Gruyter. [CC BY-NC-ND] This work is licensed under the Creative Commons Attribution-NonCommercial-NoDerivatives 4.0 International License.
https://doi.org/10.1515/9783110776232-006

makes all the more important the proper enforcement of security measures." – G. J. Ellerton, 1958.[3]

On 20 November 1952, a delegation of the UK's top intelligence officers met in Nairobi to make a plan to curb anticolonial resistance. One month before, the Governor of the Kenya Colony, Sir Evelyn Baring, had declared a State of Emergency in order to relieve his government of restrictions on its reaction to the Mau Mau Uprising.[4] Since the occupation of the British East Africa Protectorate (1895–1920), later known as Kenya Colony and Protectorate (1920–1963), peoples resisted dispossession and exploitation in a variety of ways, including the Nandi Uprising (1895–1905), the Giriama Uprising (1913–1914), the women's uprising in Murang'a (1947), and the Kolloa Affray (1950). However, the British Colonial Government (BCG) continued to authorize harsh restrictions to reinforce their rule and protect white settlers, such as with taxes, agricultural bans, and decreasing wages.[5] In response to this and other injustices, anticolonial sentiment continued to culminate and on 9 October 1952, dissidents assassinated Senior Chief Waruhiu, a key supporter of the colonial administration. This became a flashpoint for the BCG, which had previously failed to take seriously the threat to their order. To redress their ill-preparedness, the intelligence team met shortly after Baring declared the Emergency. Among the group was none other than Sir Percy Sillitoe, Director-General of MI5. Within days, the team drafted recommendations for the reorganization of intelligence services in Kenya in order to launch a counter-insurgency campaign.[6] Sillitoe suggested that Kenya Special Branch "establish a dedicated registry for intelligence records" that should span the colony.[7] This separation is where our story begins.

---

[3] TNA, FCO 141/6969, Letter, G. J. Ellerton to T. Neil, 14 October 1958.
[4] The proclamation of a State of Emergency was issued on 20 October 1952 and its declaration triggered the Emergency Regulations 1952.
[5] See Shamsul S. M. Alam, *Rethinking the Mau Mau in Colonial Kenya*, New York 2007; Cynthia Brantley, *The Giriama and Colonial Resistance in Kenya, 1800–1920*, Los Angeles 1981; Elisha Stephen Atieno-Odhiambo, 'The Formative Years: 1945–1955', in: Bethwell Allan Ogot and William Robert Ochieng' (eds.), *Decolonization and Independence in Kenya, 1940–93*, Oxford 1995, 25–47; Bethwell A. Ogot, 'Mau Mau & Nationhood: The Untold Story', in: Elisha Stephen Atieno-Odhiamo and John Lonsdale (eds.), *Mau Mau & Nationhood*, Oxford 2003, 8–36.
[6] For a fuller account of the re-organization of the intelligence services, see Randall Heather, 'Intelligence and Counter-Insurgency in Kenya, 1952–56', in: Ian Beckett (ed.), *Modern Counter-Insurgency*, London 2007, 79–106.
[7] Calder Walton, *Empire of Secrets: British Intelligence, the Cold War and the Twilight of Empire*, New York 2013, 244.

Separation is the key process in the making of secrets. Keeping a secret requires the maintenance of that separation. British attempts at secrecy characterized the Emergency in Kenya from the start until well after its end. From whom exactly the BCG kept secrets differed according to circumstance, as the following article will discuss. However, the word *attempt* is key. Awareness of detention camps, torture, and starvation campaigns existed first and foremost with those subjected to British violence during the Emergency, and those who authorized and enacted it. Further, there were those who observed it and those who read about it in reports distributed within and beyond Kenya.[8] At a certain point, keeping secrets about the Emergency was no longer just about managing awareness but about depriving potential and actual claimants of corroborating evidence. Sillitoe's suggestion, to create a dedicated registry for intelligence records, facilitated this separation by using a recordkeeping solution. When the combat of the Emergency slowed, the BCG issued its first ever regulations concerning administrative archives in order to preserve the secrecy enshrouding the BCG's documents related to the Emergency.

Eventually, the habituation of colonial secrecy in archives resulted in mass record purging in Kenya prior to political independence. In the early 1960s, British officers identified exactly those records classified in the manner described throughout this article for destruction or removal to London in order to make them inaccessible to the government and peoples of independent Kenya. This was an exercise that the UK Colonial Office authorized not only in Kenya but across the British Empire and which resulted in the formation of the so-called 'migrated archives.' These secret records came to light only in 2011 during a lawsuit wherein survivors of the Kenya Emergency sued the UK Foreign Office for damages resulting from the torture they endured. Since the release of the 'migrated archives' to the UK National Archives, historians have written about the implications of secrecy at such a scale, however, there is scant historical study of their origins.[9] The following article thus situates the 'migrated archives' in

---

[8] See for example, Fenner Brockway, *Why Mau Mau? An Analysis and a Remedy*, London 1953; George Padmore, 'Behind the Mau Mau', in: *Phylon* 14/4 (1953), 355–372; Mbiyu Koinange, *The People of Kenya Speak for Themselves*, Detroit 1955; Eileen Fletcher, *Truth about Kenya: An Eye-Witness Account*, London 1956.

[9] See Edward Hampshire, '"Apply the Flame More Searingly": The Destruction and Migration of the Archives of British Colonial Administration: A Southeast Asia Case Study', in: *The Journal of Imperial and Commonwealth History* 41/2 (2013), 334–352; Gregory Rawlings, 'Lost Files, Forgotten Papers and Colonial Disclosures: The "Migrated Archives" and the Pacific, 1963–2013', in: *The Journal of Pacific History* 50/2 (2015), 189–121; Caroline Elkins, 'Looking beyond Mau Mau: Archiving Violence in the Era of Decolonization', in: *The American Historical Review* 120/3 (2015), 852–868; Nathan Mnjama, 'Migrated Archives: The African Perspectives', in: *Jour-

their historical context as the product of a counter-insurgency wherein tight control over sensitive information formed a central part of the British Colonial Government's strategy. While the Emergency's combat ended by 1960, efforts to conceal evidence of the BCG's activities persisted.

This article begins with a discussion on the Emergency and accompanying forms of information management to show the co-evolution of intelligence systems and recordkeeping practices. It proceeds by analyzing the British bases of information during the Emergency, namely the use of tortuous screening techniques and racist paranoia, in order to contextualize the chronic ignorance that disabled the colonial administration's counter-insurgency. This is followed by an example of the official misuse of legal evidence before analyzing colonial censorship and propaganda strategies aimed at mitigating reputational loss in international fora. Finally, it examines the development of colonial archival practice as an aspect of the Emergency. In doing so, this article argues that the BCG regarded its archive as a tool to control and conceal evidence of the Emergency.

The Emergency and Information Management

Before examining the conditions in which the 'migrated archives' arose in greater detail, it is necessary to establish a context for the Emergency. I use the term "Emergency" in order to refer to the British Colonial response to anticolonial dissent in Kenya between 1952–1960. Careful not to declare war and trigger either a legal context that would have either limited or scrutinized BCG activity or create the idea that Britain had lost control in Kenya, the administration used a tactic common to the British empire and declared an emergency.[10] The Emergency manifested as a war in Kenya's central highlands between the Kenya Land and Freedom Army, often referred to as Mau Mau, and British forces that delegated much of the actual combat to the Home Guard.[11] Among the legal affordances

---

nal of the South African Society of Archivists 48 (2015), 45–54; David Phillips, 'The "Migrated Archives" and a Forgotten Corner of Empire: The British Borneo Territories', in: *The Journal of Imperial and Commonwealth History* 44/6 (2016), 1001–1019; Shohei Sato, '"Operation Legacy": Britain's Destruction and Concealment of Colonial Records Worldwide', in: *The Journal of Imperial and Commonwealth History* 45/4 (2017), 697–719.

10 See David French, *The British Way in Counter-Insurgency, 1945–1967*, Oxford 2012, who argues that the British hid the use of force in colonial counterinsurgencies behind legality.

11 The etymology of 'Mau Mau' is disputed. Writing in 1953, George Padmore argued that, "The very term 'Mau Mau' was invented by the settler Press to discredit the Africans and justify the

of an emergency were powers of search and arrest, movement restriction, curfew, censorship, restrictions on public meetings, detention, collective punishment, mass internment in prison camps, and a uniquely high use of the death penalty.[12] "Emergency" thus refers to the BCG's toolkit of repression, which incited armed self-defense from those who resisted, and it centers the BCG as the originator of the Emergency's violence.[13] The difficulty of stating how many deaths and detentions resulted from the Emergency is no accident, but itself the result of the indiscriminate use of violence, the colonial method of documentation during the Emergency, and the subsequent concealment and destruction of relevant records. However, it is estimated that British Emergency policy contained one million people in village reserves, murdered 14,000 people and led to the detention of at least 150,000 Kikuyu-speaking peoples, a uniquely high proportion of the population in comparison to other British colonial emergencies.[14] Much of the vast and impressive historiography of this period aptly discusses the moral and political economy of anti-colonial dissent in Kenya, the complexities of loyalism, and the political, cultural, and social legacies of this trauma in Kenya.[15] However, until the early 2000s, few works addressed directly the BCG's author-

---

white man's legalized terror against a once peaceful and long-suffering people." George Padmore, 'Behind the Mau Mau', 355–372. Josiah Kariuki explains "Mau Mau" may have been a linguistic anagram, commonly used by Kikuyu-speaking children, for "Uma, Uma" (meaning 'go, go') that was then embraced by the British government in order to decenter claims for land and freedom. Josiah Kariuki, 'Mau Mau' Detainee, London 1964, 48–50.

12 See John Reynolds, *Empire, Emergency and International Law*, Cambridge 2017, 138–169 and Shiraz Durrani, *Never be Silent: Publishing and Imperialism in Kenya 1884–1963*, Oxford 2006.

13 David Anderson stresses the point that by declaring an emergency and bringing in troops, the British escalated anticolonial dissent into armed combat. David Anderson, *Histories of the Hanged: Britain's Dirty War in Kenya and the End of Empire*, London 2005.

14 The figures here are based on estimates provided by Encyclopedia Britannica 'Mau Mau: Kenyan political movement', https://www.britannica.com/topic/Mau-Mau (2021–11–11) and by Juliana Appiah, Roland Mireku Yeboah and Akosua Asah-Asante, 'Architecture of Denial: Imperial Violence, the Construction of Law and Historical Knowledge during the Mau Mau Uprising, 1952–1960', in: *African Journal of Legal Studies* (2021), 1–25. The number of deaths includes those listed as both Mau Mau and loyalists, as all perished under the conditions established by the British declaration. This number is contrasted by the 100 settlers whose deaths were far more sensationalized by international and local press.

15 See Tabitha Kanogo, *Squatters and the Roots of Mau Mau, 1905–1963*, Athens 1987; Frank Furedi, *The Mau Mau war in perspective*, London 1991; David Throup, *Economic & Social Origins of Mau Mau, 1945–53*, London 1990; Greet Kershaw, *Mau Mau from Below*, Oxford 1997; Bruce Berman and John Lonsdale, *Unhappy Valley: Conflict in Kenya & Africa*, Oxford 1992.

itative role in institutionalizing and systematizing violence at this scale.[16] The mass suppression of relevant documents contributed to this omission.

The Emergency presented the British Colonial Government with a complicated puzzle. The central government wished to manage a colony-wide operation to suppress Mau Mau and the wider anticolonial sentiment developing in Kenya, which was of special concern to white European settlers. However, the task required a more sophisticated understanding of its enemy than the BCG had. The racism which facilitated colonial domination produced a general narrative of Mau Mau which was unhelpful in launching targeted military action but served rather to intensify and magnify the use of indiscriminate violence. Parliament at this time, conservative-led, was running out of positive spins for British violence across the empire and anti-imperialism was growing in its base across the UK as it was globally. The BCG therefore had to control the type of information it provided to the international and British press as well as Parliament in order to maintain legitimacy in the colonies or at least to strategically decline as an imperial power.[17] To redress ignorance, the BCG invested in developing its intelligence operations across Kenya. To cope with Parliament, the BCG introduced complicated systems of control over what kind of information circulated outside of the colony regarding the Emergency. Colonial recordkeeping was, in part, an attempt to control these circuits of communication and their material consequences. By making more transparent the processes by which information and intelligence developed and the ways in which they were used by the British Colonial Government, this article establishes the body of records that would later be known as the 'migrated archives' as a function of colonial power.

Secrets formed one part of the BCG's information management strategy during the Emergency, which included the production and controlled circulation of "propaganda", "information", and "intelligence".[18] These terms did not operate

---

16 See David Anderson, *Histories of the Hanged*, London 2005 and Caroline Elkins, *Britain's Gulag: The Brutal End of Empire in Kenya*, London 2005.
17 Susan Carruthers shows how the BCG not only created its own publicity material but attempted to shape how international media represented the Emergency. Susan Carruthers, *Winning Hearts and Minds: British Governments, the Media and Colonial Counter-Insurgency, 1944 – 1960*, London 1995.
18 Psychological warfare can be understood as the "planned use of propaganda to influence enemy audiences in times of war." It is typically understood as a tactic separate from physical combat. However, in the Kenyan Emergency, the campaign for the 'hearts and minds' of an international public resulted in the suppression of records documenting colonial violence. Recordkeeping practices during the Emergency can thus be understood as situated between psychological warfare and physical combat as the logic determining which records to conceal and which to reveal. See "psychological warfare" entry in Nicholas J. Cull, David Culbert, David Welch (eds.),

with stable definitions, neither to those employing them *in situ* nor in the following discussion. This fluidity lends understanding to the eventual attempt to comprehensively remove records from Kenya to London that dealt with the Emergency. Still, distinguishing between them helps clarify the originating context for the 'migrated archives'.

According to the UK Ministry of Defence's explanation of psychological warfare, "information" is "the free communication of facts favourable or unfavourable, with no undue effort to sway the judgement of the audience." "Propaganda" is "the communication of selected information with the aim of leaving a definite impression and possibly inducing action." "Intelligence" should include "accurate and complete information about the enemy's psychological weaknesses."[19] The clarity of these definitions emanating from the Ministry of Defence is misleading as are the apparent distinct intentions behind the use of each, as will be elaborated further in the following, especially regarding the blurriness between "information" and "propaganda". However, they illustrate the BCG's *attempts* to control the flow and impact of information within Kenya and beyond within the context of a counter-insurgency in order to establish and control one legitimate perspective on the Emergency.[20] "Information" and "propaganda" refer to the BCG public messaging, which contrasted the concealed realities of the Emergency. It was in this context, through protecting bad intel in a dirty war, that not just what would become the 'migrated archives' originated but the overall design and regulation of Kenyan colonial archives.[21]

This article situates the 'migrated archives,' whose ownership is contested between Kenya and Great Britain, in its original context. The bulk of the records which were covertly removed from Kenya upon independence pertain to the Emergency period were created by the Ministry of Defence. The operation to remove and destroy documents that the British Colonial Government deemed 'embarrassing' assumed a similar logic as in the documents' creation: security of intelligence and concealing the BCG's own role in the Emergency. This article identifies several key components of colonial knowledge, including its founda-

---

Propaganda and Mass Persuasion: A Historical Encyclopedia, 1500 to the Present, Santa Barbara 2003, 323–326.
19 TNA, DEFE 28/184, "Psychological Warfare Organization", 1953–1959.
20 See David Welch, 'Propaganda, Definitions of', in: Cull, Culbert, Welch (eds.), *Propaganda and Mass Persuasion*, 317–323.
21 This chapter uses the term 'migrated archives' in order to refer to the documents stored in secret by the UK's Foreign and Commonwealth, which comprise thousands of files removed from 37 former colonies during the period of decolonization (1960–1994). Their disclosure is the result of the Mau Mau Case (2012).

tions, forms and functions, in order to contextualize what would become the 'migrated archives' as a core dimension of the BCG's Emergency efforts.

Screening and Superstition: Bases of British Colonial Knowledge during the Emergency

In July 1954, at age 15, Jane Muthoni Mara was arrested for being a "Mau Mau sympathizer" because of her work coordinating food supplies and laundry services for traveling freedom fighters as they passed through her family's village in the Embu District. Following her arrest, Jane was brought to Gatithi screening camp where a British District Officer ordered Kenyan guards to beat her and the other detainees in the hopes that torture would produce Mau Mau intel.[22] In her legal testimony fifty-six years later, Jane recalled:

> I was screaming and resisting and trying to wriggle and free myself from the men who were holding me down. Suddenly Edward produced a glass soda bottle. Waikanja told him to push the bottle into my vagina which he did. I felt excruciating pain and then realised that the glass bottle contained very hot water. Edward literally forced the bottle into me with the sole of his foot while Waikanja was looking on and directing him.[23]

In addition to beating and sexual violence, the torture techniques in screening included using hot spades to brand detainees and pliers to castrate male prisoners. Despite the extreme efforts of the screening officer, Jane refused to share information regarding the identities of any Mau Mau. As a result, she was detained for three more years. By focusing on documents, it is all too easy to forget the human harm behind the making and maintaining of the 'migrated archives'. Jane went on to play a key role in the ultimate release of the 'migrated archives', records inscribed with the violence inflicted on her and so many others.

From the onset of the Emergency, screening was the process by which a coalition of British security forces, European settlers, and the Kenya police attempted, often through force, to get information from a Mau Mau suspect and/or to persuade them to confess their own affiliation.[24] In her work on the screening camps, historian Caroline Elkins identifies Christopher Todd, the first settler ap-

---

[22] Mara, J. M. (Nov. 2010). *Jane Muthoni Mara, Witness Statement*, URL: https://www.leighday.co.uk/LeighDay/media/LeighDay/documents/Mau Mau/Claimant statements/Jane-Muthoni-Mara-WS-Final-.pdf (2015–05–10).
[23] Ibid.
[24] Elkins, *Britain's Gulag*, 63.

pointed as a screening officer, as one of the architects of the process. A two-time veteran of both world wars, Todd resumed his residency in Kenya's Rift Valley in 1950. Together with other white settlers, Todd formed a Vigilance Committee, which took, in his own words, "the law into their own hands for the purpose of protecting the lives of their families should the occasion arise."[25] Rather than penalize this self-organized gang of settlers, Governor Baring recruited Todd into his government to participate in the design and execution of screenings in order to extend Crown protection to the vigilante and to benefit from his local "knowledge" and enthusiasm.

Todd was also regarded as an asset by the British Colonial Government because of his self-professed expertise in identifying Mau Mau. Regarding the basis of recognition, Todd later stated, "There was something about the ideas and whole demeanor, an aura of evil which emanated from the man or woman which showed the state of utter degradation to which a once normal human being had been reduced [...]."[26] Todd's description reflected a general (mis)understanding of Mau Mau. Described as a 'disease' or psychological state of madness which spread amongst Kenyans, though mainly Kikuyu, Mau Mau was declared an inhumane condition beset upon the already atavistic Black peoples in Kenya. Historian of British Colonial Administration and friend of Governor Baring, Margery Perham, described the Emergency as an attempt to "break the spell of the Mau Mau."[27] Here Perham expressed British colonial ignorance of the powerful anticolonial movement through mystification. Chinua Achebe describes this as a "perception problem", in which the European othering of the Black African was deliberately invented to better facilitate colonial domination.[28]

Fatal Costs of Flimsy Evidence

The Emergency itself was announced on 20 October 1952 and launched in the early morning hours of the following day with a mass arrest. Hoping to decapitate the anticolonial movement, Operation Jock Scott targeted over 140 individuals believed by the British to be the political leadership of Mau Mau and ordered for their capture and arrest. The strategy, however, miscalculated the role played by the detained individuals, many of whom were not at all connected

---

25 C. T. Todd, *Kenya's Red Sunset*, 240, RH: MSS Afr s. 917.
26 Todd, *Kenya's Red Sunset*, 263.
27 Kariuki, *"Mau Mau" Detainee*, 14.
28 Chinua Achebe, *Africa's Tarnished Name*, London 2018.

to and others still explicitly opposed Mau Mau.[29] Jomo Kenyatta, one of the most esteemed of Kikuyu political leadership, was among those arrested. President elect of the Kenya Africa Union and champion of Kikuyu nationalism; Kenyatta was thought by the BCG to be the head of Mau Mau. Kenyatta's threat as head of the anticolonial movement was so powerful to the British that his personal library, journals, writings, and collected artifacts were seized at the time of his arrest thereby erasing material evidence of his intellect and stealing the cultural objects he had collected throughout the African diaspora. His arrest and trial, however, were based on flimsy and purchased evidence.

New African political leadership in Kenya rivaled the authority of chiefs and former hierarchical distributions of social authority. As such, African informants became strategically available to the British for a price – both financial and political (with the hopes of restoring/maintaining the power of the chief over new ethnic nationalists, such as Kenyatta). Historian Charles Douglas-Home suggests that at the time of Kenyatta's accusation, only a promise of reward would incentivize an African witness to provide evidence against Kenyatta.[30] The trial resulted in the imprisonment of Kenyatta along with the rest of the Kapenguria Six, the name given to the most famous of those arrested during Operation Jock Scott, despite the lack of compelling evidence that the six were essential, or even related, to Mau Mau operations. The trial demonstrated the value of bad evidence: if it promised to assist in dismantling the anticolonial threat and to maintain the image of British right-doing, the government would authorize its use.[31]

The trial not only failed in putting the brakes on Mau Mau but marked the intensification of fatal violence during the Emergency because the BCG had gravely misunderstood Mau Mau's structure and aims. It was neither a contagious psychosis nor a terrorist army dependent on hierarchical leadership. Thousands of Mau Mau militants fled to the forests after the trial where they formed armies. Without comparable area expertise, the British Colonial Government resorted to air strikes to combat the forest armies, resulting in deaths of unknown numbers. Just as the terrain, the relationship between Mau Mau, Kikuyu and other politicized groups across the colony eluded the British government. The colonial knowledge which facilitated administrative dominance had homogenized the many peoples of Kenya into ethnic groups to which the British attributed different physiological, moral, and intellectual traits. These categories failed to explain the crisis their government faced yet color the documentary traces

---

29 Anderson, *Histories of the Hanged*, 62.
30 Charles Douglas-Home, *Evelyn Baring: The Last Proconsul*, Glasgow 1978, 246–248.
31 See Berman and Lonsdale, *Unhappy Valley* and Anderson, *Histories of the Hanged* for the many ways in which colonial authorities manipulated legal systems throughout the Emergency.

they left behind. It was in this context that the violent screening processes began, to compensate for the limitations of colonial knowledge without ever acknowledging them as such. However, Huw Bennett, the first historian to make use of the 'migrated archives' in narrating the history of British counter-insurgency in Kenya, argues that the British never succeeded in identifying who actually comprised Mau Mau.[32] The realities of Mau Mau and other Kenyan peoples who opposed the colonial government were not as important or instructive to British counter-insurgency as what the BCG perceived to be or projected as their aims and therefore are not decipherable in the records that form the 'migrated archives'.[33] The Emergency empowered strategies of colonial ignorance.

Perception Control via Censorship and Propaganda

The growing crisis in Kenya presented a difficult public relations challenge to the colonial government: how to spin a story that sympathized with, even valorized the British administration despite the escalation of authorized violence during the Emergency? Civil servant and soon-to-be Emergency apologist, F. D. Corfield described the challenge as conducting an autocracy within the colony and justifying it to a democratic Parliament that had no experience with, in his words, "primitive peoples".[34] Still, popular opinion was essential to the maintenance of political legitimacy and, as pointed out by historian Joanna Lewis, official propaganda and censorship – their uses established and exploited in the second world war – were the preferred tools.[35]

Faced with the task of delivering a speech to Parliament regarding the Emergency just one week into Kenyatta's trial, Secretary of State for the Colonies Sir Anthony Eden wrote to Governor Baring:

> Your telegram provided useful material about numbers detained and charged but I would be grateful for latest available figures both for those arrested after initial screening and of those detained under Emergency regulations. In particular I will be asked about numbers

---

[32] Huw Bennett, *Fighting the Mau Mau: The British Army and Counter-Insurgency in the Kenya Emergency*, Cambridge 2013, 3.
[33] David French, *The British Way in Counter-Insurgency: 1945–1967*, Oxford 2011, 58.
[34] TNA, FCO 141/6576, Drafted letter from F. D. Corfield, 21 November 1958.
[35] Joanna Lewis, '"Daddy Wouldn't Buy Me a Mau Mau": The British Popular Press and the Demoralization of Empire', in: E. S. Atieno Odhiambo and John Londsdale (eds.), *Mau Mau and Nationhood: Arms, Authority and Narration*, Oxford 2003, 228.

detained without having been charged with any criminal offence. Is there any information in general terms (i.e. not referring to individuals) which I can use about latter other than that which you have already provided. I notice from press reports that some murderers are about to be hanged at Thomson's Falls. In view of previous publicity about detainees being herded in sight of the gallows there, may I assume precautions will be taken to ensure executions are not REPEAT NOT public. Details of arrangements to achieve this might prove useful.[36]

Eden's telegram, dispatched as a cypher and marked with a bright purple 'CONFIDENTIAL' stamp, indicates the contradictory circuits of communication that colonial intelligence would have to navigate during the Emergency. On the one hand, Baring's office was required to collect and distribute statistical information regarding detainees and their charges and later death/casualty tolls as a kind of progress report for Whitehall's consideration but on the other hand, his government would have to censor the realities behind these statistics such as the hangings mentioned here. As a result, the central colonial government in Kenya instructed the provincial and district offices to collect and record numerical information regarding the deaths, casualties, and arrests. In fact, the reports do not even offer 'Mau Mau' as an identifying category for victims of Emergency decree. Rather, the dead and wounded were described only in their quantity.

The BCG in Kenya strategized public perception via propaganda and censorship concurrent to developing their systems of intelligence. During Kenyatta's trial, in December of 1952, MI5 sent a delegate to Nairobi responsible for the reorganization of the colony's Intelligence Department.[37] On December 19, 1952 Governor Baring invited A. M. MacDonald of the U.K. Security Service to the post of Intelligence Adviser to the Kenya Government for one year. According to the invitation, the post would require MacDonald to organize the collection of intelligence, coordinate the work of all intelligence agencies within the colony, and promote collaboration with Special Branches in neighboring territories. In addition to appointing MacDonald to reorganize the Kenya Special Police Forces and systematize intelligence gathering, Governor Baring ordered the development of a Kenya Intelligence Committee, responsible at the provincial level for collecting and advising on matters of intelligence. This structural overhaul triggered the formalization of intelligence infrastructure across the colony. The colonial government thereby self-fashioned itself to the metropole without describ-

---

[36] TNA, FCO 141/7212, Decoded telegram from Secretary of State to Governor in Nairobi, 11 December 1952.
[37] TNA, FCO 141/6522, Letter from the Governor's Office to MacDonald, 19 December 1952.

ing the fatal violence or the torture techniques employed during the Emergency whilst attempting to develop protected channels for an information flow to facilitate counter-insurgency.

The formation and purview of the committee was not entirely thanks to Governor Baring's idea and MacDonald's execution. Two years before the formal declaration of the Emergency in Kenya, James Griffiths – Secretary of the State for the Colonies at the time, circulated a report amongst BCG offices across the empire on lessons learned from the Emergency in Malaya. Among the *first* of these lessons was the significance of instating systems of intelligence, coming after the establishment of a police force and before creating a legislative context which provides the colonial government any authority deemed necessary for their purposes. Griffiths wrote, "complete agreement exists that the first essential for the prevention of emergencies, and for dealing with them if they should occur, is a regular and efficient system for information and intelligence."[38] Historian Rory Cormac argues that the escalation of anticolonialism across the British empire, not only in Kenya, intensified the significance of colonial security in the eyes of Whitehall and that, especially in the Cold War context, this elevated the significance of systems of intelligence and information management.[39]

Kenya's Intelligence Committee had its first meeting in 1953 under the direction of A. M. MacDonald during which the organization's role was further clarified. The committee was responsible for obtaining and providing 'operational intelligence.' MacDonald elaborated, this meant: a) providing information about an area for commanders immediately prior to operations in that area, b) enabling action to be taken to intervene in terrorist activity or at least to be on the spot as soon as possible after incidents, and c) briefing units entering an area on the local situation.[40] In other words, the committee should establish contacts, informants, or surveillance such that they could in turn prescribe strategic military action to the central government according to British interests. The desire to create channels for information flow brought the BCG to prioritize relations with loyalists, on whom they depended for any route to intel.[41]

---

[38] TNA, FCO 141/6540, Circular Dispatch, "Internal Security: Lessons of the Emergency in Malaya", James Griffiths, 11 July 1950.
[39] Rory Cormac, *Confronting the Colonies: British Intelligence and Counterinsurgency*, New York 2013, 5.
[40] TNA, FCO 141/5641, Minutes of first Meeting, Kenya Intelligence Committee, 12 February 1953.
[41] Shiraz Durrani's work shows how Mau Mau used the BCG's reliance on loyalists to their advantage through infiltration and subversion. For example, tailors created white arm bands similar to those used by the Home Guard for Mau Mau in order to support double-agents. Durrani, *Never be Silent*, 166.

In the second meeting of the Kenya Intelligence Committee on 25 February 1953, MacDonald led the committee to agree that "there was little chance of obtaining immediate information of incidents in progress until there were sufficient loyal Africans on the ground [via] the proper and rapid expansion of the Home Guard."[42] In the Cold War period, forming militias of local peoples was commonplace in combating emerging nationalism.[43] Early on in the Emergency, the BCG created different "information" strategies according to four different groups: the loyalists, the "waverers", active supporters of Mau Mau living in reserves, and forest fighters.[44] Several common themes cut through the messaging to all four, such as the emphasis that "there was in effect a civil war and that the struggle was not black versus white."[45] This point tried to shift the focus from the BCG to the Home Guards as Mau Mau's enemy, an enduring tactic in the BCG's evasion of responsibility for the violence of the Emergency. However, General George Erskine and Governor Baring were the responsible individuals for authorizing all military measures during the Emergency.[46] Active in the years of most concentrated violence (1953–1955), the Home Guards were responsible for watching over Kikuyu reserves, conducting anti-Mau Mau sweeps, penetrating forest fighter groups, and engaging in armed combat.[47] Among their duties in the villages, the Home Guards were armed with megaphones to serve as a mouthpiece for the BCG's campaign in anti-Mau Mau psychological warfare.

Just one month after the declaration of Emergency, MacDonald emphasized the utility of psychological warfare campaigns in fighting Mau Mau. On 26 November 1952, a meeting was convened at the Government House in order to discuss the Emergency and preliminary actions the administration should take. In

---

42 TNA, FCO 141/5641, Minutes of second meeting, Kenya Intelligence Committee, 25 February 1953.
43 See for example David Anderson and David Branch (eds.), *Allies at the End of Empire: Loyalists, Nationalists and the Cold War, 1945–76*, New York 2018.
44 This example helps to illustrate the BCG's blurred lines between "information" and "propaganda". This typology was established by the Information Working Party, which agreed that, "The Information problem is different for each of these classes, but, with the possible exception of the gangsters in the forests, they are so intermingled that it is difficult, if not impossible, to direct information to any one class by itself. For this reason it is felt to be wrong to separate 'psychological warfare' from normal information work [...]" TNA, FCO 141/6586, Extract from Note on Information to the Kikuyu, Embu and Meru in Central Province, 24 September 1953.
45 TNA, FCO 141/6586, African Information Working Party Minutes, 25 September 1953.
46 As summarized by Erskine himself in his report, "The Kenya Emergency. June 1953–May 1955", TNA, FCO 141/6540.
47 Daniel Branch, 'The Enemy Within: Loyalists and the War Against Mau Mau in Kenya', in: *Journal of African History* 48 (2007), 291–315.

attendance was son-of-missionaries anthropologist Louis Leakey who agreed to draft a statement condemning Mau Mau in order to drum up support by the Kikuyu for the BCG. Leakey would ask Eliud Mathu, the first Black member of the Legislative Council of Kenya, and Harry Thuku to sign the statement as an act of revival for the moderate Kikuyu Provincial Association. MacDonald ordered that such a statement be "splashed" through the press and radios as the first official act of propaganda during the Emergency.[48] Over the next three years, the BCG attempted a smear campaign against Mau Mau in the Emergency through control over vernacular press, whisper campaigns, sky shouting, broadcasting and photographic services, "mobile information" vans, and traveling megaphone announcements.[49]

An Information Working Party formed in September 1953 and was responsible for identifying audience groups for BCG's propaganda and soliciting relevant messages from the intelligence committee. Each class, according to the working party, required a tailored approach, but they agreed on the following universal messaging: 1) Mau Mau is an evil thing 2) It is Africans' responsibility to destroy Mau Mau 3) The British Administration is in the best interest of Kenya and all its inhabitants. Otherwise, the Information Working Party specified that messaging towards loyalists should emphasize that "they are on the winning side" and they "need not fear their position will be undermined by the return of subversive leaders." To the waverers, the working party wanted to "show that the loyalists are the future leaders." Lastly, to the "gangsters", the working party wished to emphasize "the growing revulsion of feeling against them."[50] The propagation of this "information" was accompanied by ongoing repression of vernacular press, which circulated printed anticolonial critique. The working party's messaging, across the board, omitted mention of the BCG itself, except for as the bastion of "law and order."[51] It thus aimed to make unknown the colonial administration's role in the Emergency and eradicate public discourse that showed otherwise.

---

48 TNA, FCO 141/6522, Minutes of meeting held at Government House, 26 November 1952.
49 The discussion of this 'hearts and minds' campaign was accompanied by other strategies such as levying taxes against Kikuyu, the use of vomit gas, rifle-fire and the death penalty. The smear campaign was thus one tool in a wider set of emergency strategies. TNA, FCO 141/6586, Record of a meeting Held at Government House on 26th November 1952 to Discuss Certain Matters Connected with the Present Emergency, 26 November 1952.
50 TNA, FCO 141/6586, Extract from note on information to the Kikuyu, Embu and Meru in Central Province, taken from Director of Information's Personal File on Information Working Party, 24 September 1953.
51 Ibid.

The Information Working Party was an offshoot of the Kenya Information Office (KIO), an organization which developed in 1940 at the start of WWII. The office was responsible for distributing wartime news to settler and administrative communities across Kenya. At the war's end, the *Report of the Development Committee* suggested that the KIO transition into an "Information Service for Africans".[52] As such, it reorganized its services in 1946 to include producing publications (news, periodicals, pamphlets and booklets), daily vernacular broadcasts, commercially produced and distributed photographic prints, and some films that were shown by KIO's officers in charge of cinema vans, all of which were deliberately made to promote British interests. In 1953, KIO offered its information services and infrastructure to the Emergency effort in order, according to their self-authored institutional history "to use propaganda methods to help restore peace and form sound opinion amongst Africans in the disaffected...areas of the Colony."[53] The Information Working Party produced records to circulate publicly within Kenya in order to try and manipulate public opinion and incite action against Mau Mau. Its title thus blurred the distinction between information and propaganda. Distinctions were rather made on the basis of who could know or prove what, and who could be privy to which kinds of information. For this, recordkeeping practices were central to the Emergency in order to regulate which messages the BCG advanced and what evidence it withdrew.

Security of Documents and the Colonial Development of Archival Practice

That the British Colonial Government in Kenya felt its own precarity during the Emergency is evident in its anxious obsession with recordkeeping. With faltering confidence in legitimacy, systems of rule took on new meaning. If the administration could outline and abide by rules within the protective measures of bureaucracy, then they surely had not strayed too far from their claims to modernity and civilization. Additionally, the delicacy of the Emergency encouraged the colonial administration to tighten security control in all realms. Lonsdale observes:

> ...the Emergency was a powerful weapon of bureaucratic politics with which administrators could attempt to reverse the decline of their prestige and authority in relation to the technical departments and overcome the growing breach with the central administration[54]

---

52 TNA, FCO 141/6586, Circular, "History of Department of Information", n.d.
53 Ibid.
54 Berman and Lonsdale, *Unhappy Valley*, 253.

These bureaucratic politics were articulated through paperwork, as though order on the page would yield order in the colony. The carefully collected intelligence had to be first gathered and then protected: restricting access and use of sensitive records was a part of the Emergency-effort. This section historicizes the development of colonial archival practice from 1928 through the Emergency in order to clarify the archive's function(s) to power.

In 1928, a new filing system was introduced by the Honorable Chief Native Commissioner in Kenya in order to more efficiently and usefully manage the storage and therefore accessibility of communication within Kenya and other British colonies. The Commissioner reported at the time of the instructions that it was estimated that 33 percent of clerks across the colony were spending an entire day looking for files, which should be found, according to him, in 30 seconds or less. Better (and faster) recordkeeping seemed to be the key to not only managing the information produced by colonial rule but the actual work of governance. Thus, the memorandum emphasized the organization and retrieval of current records. For non-current records, or those which had not been used for at least twelve months, the instructions stated that: "all old files should be marked 'ARCHIVES' in red ink, and reference should be made on them to any subsequent volumes opened."[55] Thereby enforcing a retention schedule, or method by which records were selected for archival preservation or destruction, in which *every single file* should be preserved. The British government paid more specific attention to the archives across the colonies when the fragility of its empire was no longer possible to ignore.

In December 1948, amidst the emergence of independent nations out of the British empire, the colonial Secretariat addressed all heads of Department in Kenya regarding the importance of proper preservation of records that might be of historical interest. The archive was no longer just a dumping ground for the growing piles of 'old' and unused files, but the foundation on which the British Empire would be memorialized. In October 1955, a set of *Draft Rules and Regulations for the Management and Control of all Archives of the Central Government* was circulated across the Kenya Colony. The timing of these rules, the first of its kind issued in Kenya, corresponded with an apparent dwindling in the active combat in the Emergency and the reorganization by the UK of its intelligence services during the early Cold War.[56] These instructions introduced a new retention schedule that specified the kinds of documents that should be preserved. The list of record-types illustrated the colonial ideal of well-organized and

---

55 KNA, DC/Lamu/2/12/16, Memorandum, "Filing Instructions", 19 January 1929.
56 See Christopher Andrew, *The Defence of the Realm,* London 2009, 319–329.

well-documented rule. The first chief archivist in Kenya appointed in 1956, Evelyn Bwye, asserted that the colonial archive should "serve the practical purposes of administration by providing precedents and historical background to government business in the shape of old departmental files and administrative reports."[57] As indicated by the Intelligence Committee, the practical purposes of the Kenyan colonial administration in 1955 did not necessitate historical background from its archives as much as strategic control. Managing the colonial government's archives in Kenya during the 1950s was a matter of protecting intelligence for internal reference and possible future use. From the start of the 1950s onwards, the recordkeeping principle most exercised across colonial governments was the protection of counter-insurgency documents.

By April 22, 1953 the Kenya Intelligence Committee had begun to install Security Officers across administrative departments in order to enforce security precautions regarding classified information.[58] The previous year, the British Government introduced a "special procedure" to vet the reliability of all Civil Servants in Kenya who "might have access in the course of their duties to information of an exceptionally secret or delicate kind."[59] The vetting process involved the Special Branch conducting a background check based on intelligence gathered on an individual basis for every nominee to work within BCG or existing employees facing promotion.[60] Once the matter of personnel was clarified, the Kenya Intelligence Committee, together with the Cabinet Office and Ministry for Defence considered further protective measures for sensitive information. These measures included the use of a classification schema for all documents, access and storage of classified documents, transport and encryption of secret communication, and destruction and/or disposal of records. The classification schema consisted of four security grades, here listed in descending order of sensitivity: 'Top Secret', 'Secret', 'Confidential' and 'Restricted'. To further complicate things, BCG introduced three subgroups for classified documents: 'Personal', 'Guard', and 'U.K. Eyes Only'. These labels further indicated rules of access. For example, 'Personal' files were not to be seen by non-officials, not even by elected ministers. 'Guard' materials were specifically forbidden to share with a national of the United States of America. 'U.K. Eyes Only' files were only for members of the Home or Overseas Civil Service, Foreign Service or Armed

---

57 KNA, AJ/1/17, Letter from Bwye to Charman, 4 September 1963.
58 TNA, FCO 141/5641, Minutes of sixth meeting, Kenya Intelligence Committee, 22 April 1953.
59 TNA, FCO 141/6998, Letter from G H Webb to Miss Pontet, 20 March 1962.
60 TNA, FCO 141/6998, Memorandum, "Security Vetting – East Africa, Appointments – Security Vetting of Government Officers – Office of the Chief Secretary", n.d.

Forces.[61] Beyond their intended viewership, these grades corresponded to appropriate modes of transport and storage.

The BCG attempted to articulate and enforce strict mechanisms of control over their sensitive records. The directive *Material Security Protection for Classified Information in Government Offices* described the ideal condition for storing such documents across government offices in Kenya. For example, they should be kept locked in steel filing cabinets secured to the wall. An appointed security officer should keep the key on his person at all times. These cabinets, it was instructed, should be stored in locked windowless strong rooms, the doors of which should be reinforced on the outside by steel plating.[62] Identified as "Key Points," these strong rooms, the BCG insisted, should be seen as important to the Emergency such that their "destruction or damage would impair either the general or local war effort." [63] When it was necessary to transport or communicate classified information, the grading indicated how to do so most cautiously. For example, Top Secret material was ordered to be transmitted in a container fastened by a combination padlock and carried by an authorized European "safe hand".[64] Telegrams were encrypted using the Kenyan police code and sent to the Cypher Office for deciphering. For oral transmission, colonial officials were reminded of "common sense precautions", that they should always keep in mind offices with ill-fitting doors, thin partition walls or open fanlights to better avoid eavesdropping.[65] In 1958, G. J. Ellerton, Permanent Secretary of Defence, summarized the anxieties of interception: "We know that certain people have realized the possibilities and advantages of penetrating the Government's secrets. This is a threat to security which is bound to increase and makes all the more important the proper enforcement of security measures."[66] Record storage was the BCG's attempt to maintain Emergency secrets. The archive did not simply preserve records of the Emergency but was a technology of concealment.

The BCG's elaborate mechanisms of document security were fragile and regularly breached. Throughout the Emergency, colonial offices tracked the movement of classified files, called accountable documents, that detailed sensitive matters in order to best ensure they never fell into the wrong hands. Postal work-

---

61 TNA, FCO 141/6998, Letter from Magor to Heads of Ministries, 23 April 1958.
62 TNA, FCO 141/6998, Memorandum, "Basic standards of material security protection for classified information in government offices", n.d.
63 Ibid.
64 TNA, FCO 141/6969, Letter, Magor to Private Secretary to the Governor, "Security of Decyphered and Decoded Telegrams," 14 October 1959.
65 Ibid.
66 TNA, FCO 141/6969, Letter from Ellerton to Neil, 14 October 1958.

ers transported accountable documents in nested protective layers. In 1959, an African postal worker unhappy with their working conditions in Nairobi threatened to deliberately misdirect confidential mail to newspapers in the United States and the U.S.S.R. causing the Governor's office stress over the effectiveness of their security.[67] In August of the same year, Tom Mboya, at a Nairobi People's Convention party, claimed that a confidential source gave him copies of cables between the Secretary of State for the Colonies and the Kenyan Governor that detailed the plans to develop a constitution for an independent Kenya.[68] Throughout the Emergency, Special Branch cultivated and relied on an extensive informant network that was infiltrated by Mau Mau. The inability to ascertain who was a saboteur and who was not increased the BCG's suspicion of all Africans, especially those employed by the government.

Despite the BCG's investment in document security measures, a number of factors rendered them defective. The extent of colonial ignorance produced a paranoia of Africans, especially Kikuyu-speaking peoples, yet the BCG relied heavily on loyalists in the counter-insurgency campaign. Historian John Lonsdale argues that though "official knowledge was distorted by racial separation; opaque and partial, it served the interests of their African informants [...]."[69] Thus, despite its attempts to establish a "communications monopoly", the BCG was not equipped to prevent the "soldier-information worker" network of the Mau Mau and their sympathizers.[70] Reports of redirected mail resulted in the BCG's administrative secretary overseeing that "a European Police courier system [replace] the former Kikuyu postman on all routes" in 1955. However, four years later, in the last weeks of the Emergency, the BCG was still registering complaints of interception.[71] While the military campaign was largely over, the BCG was nowhere near finished fighting for the control of information related to the Emergency.

---

67 TNA, FCO 141/6969, Decoded telegram from Governor from Secretary of State, "Interference with Post Articles", 6 July 1959.
68 TNA, FCO 141/6969, Circular Report from Colony Protective Security Officer, "Report on Suspected Leakage of Information", n.d.
69 Berman and Lonsdale, *Unhappy Valley*, 284.
70 Shiraz Durrani uses these phrases to identify repression of vernacular press as one way that the BCG tried to eliminate all perspectives but its own through a "communications monopoly", and how one of the ways Mau Mau resisted this was the formation of "soldier-information workers", who performed many and varied tasks in order to collect, store, and make available intelligence from different units, both internal to Mau Mau and through infiltration of the BCG. Durrani, *Never be Silent*.
71 TNA, FCO 141/6969, Letter, Magor to Private Secretary to the Governor, "Security of Decyphered and Decoded Telegrams", 14 October 1959.

Intelligence breaches were not only the result of anticolonial intention but also of colonial neglect. In October of 1958, G. J. Ellerton wrote to Thomas Neil, who by now was the leading Security Officer, complaining of security weaknesses in the administration. Ellerton criticized his colleagues for leaving classified papers on their desks unsupervised, of misclassifying documents, and for forgetting to read and abide by the Government's Kenya Security Instructions.[72] Neil sprang into action, contacting all heads of departments regarding their preparedness for interception. He wanted to know: how quickly could the offices of British Colonial Government destroy all of their classified materials should the occasion arise?[73] His survey, completed in 1958, would become the basis of 'Operation Legacy,' the coordinated approach to destroy and remove any record which the British Colonial Government suspected would disturb the transition to independence and reveal the nature of its counter-insurgency.

Conclusion

The 1955 *Rules and Regulations for the Management and Control of all Archives* made explicit the difference established by the BCG between "archives" and the amassing classified documents throughout the colony. Prefacing its introduction, the text asserted: "these Rules and Regulations do not apply to CLASSIFIED DOCUMENTS which should be dealt with strictly in accordance with existing directives regarding [...] SECURITY REGULATIONS"[74] Classified documents, as has been addressed in this article, mostly had to do with the activities of the British Colonial Government throughout the Emergency. The records detail the way in which the BCG developed its own perception of Mau Mau and the Kenyan population in order to fatally eliminate the radical anticolonial threat. They are the evidence of different circuits of communication, constructed with the desire to control the perception of the Emergency – in Parliament and in the colony. Their concealment functioned to obscure the BCG's role in authorizing systematic violence. By making these records inaccessible, the BCG attempted to avoid consequences for their dirty war.

By historicizing the circumstances in and processes through which the Kenyan 'migrated archives' formed, this article assists in making more transparent the conditions of their enduring concealment. Within imperial historiography,

---

[72] TNA, FCO 141/6969, Letter from Ellerton to Neil, 14 October 1958.
[73] TNA, FCO 141/6971, Assorted letters related to distributed survey "Destruction of Classified Documents".
[74] KNA, AJ/1/17, Archives Circular No 1, "Archives Rules and Regulations", 1955.

scholars often critique the biases and tones of settlers and colonists that compose sources.[75] However, as this article shows, it is not only in their content but through their formation that colonial archives service imperial power. Formed on the basis of racist ignorance, the colonial government dealt with Kenyan Emergency records with a secrecy that did not expire with political independence. In order to more fruitfully deal with the power imbued in the sources historians turn to in order to reconstruct the British colonial past, at least those authored and organized by colonial administrations, it is necessary to examine recordkeeping itself as a practice of colonial domination. In the case of this article, that includes the value of false evidence in service of imperial interests, practices of censorship and propaganda to protect reputations and control populations, and archival secrecy practiced on racialized lines. In other words, the provenance of the Kenyan 'migrated archives' can be understood as the protection of bad intel in a dirty war, a purpose they served as late as 2011.

---

75 See for example, Toyin Falola and Christian Jennings, *Sources and Methods in African History: Spoken Written Unearthed*, Rochester, NY 2004.

Forum

Johannes Paulmann
Researching the History of Social Differentiation and Human Categorization

Social differentiations and human categorizations are subject to historical change: this applies to the arrangement into estates, classes or strata as well as to the division into large social fields such as politics, religion or society itself. Social entities such as groups, networks or organisations also show different historical characteristics and change. The following considerations provide an overview of the historiographical study of differentiation processes. The introduction uses the example of religious-confessional differentiations to show the relationships between theoretical orientation, historical developments and epochal divisions in European history (1). The essay then explains the perspectives from which historical scholarship in Germany has researched both long-term developments and time- and space-specific forms of differentiation since the 1960s: from the perspective of the functional differentiation of social sub-areas (2.), as stratificational differentiation in the sense of social inequality of population groups (3.) and as socio-cultural differentiation through the formation of communities (4.). Furthermore, it has drawn on a concept of intersectionality that combines stratificational differentiation and differentiation through the formation of communities, and historicised it (5.). These perspectives are based on different assumptions regarding epochal divisions and concepts of historical change (especially from pre-modernity to modernity) and often on an understanding of society that assumes European lines of development for all societies in the world. Moreover, they take into account historical processes, structures and the actions of players in different ways. And they are relevant for the interpretation of the present. Finally, historical anthropology is presented as a research perspective (6.). It opens up the view of how people in the past distinguished themselves from one another by naming, marking, establishing and trying to preserve differences from others, or – on the contrary – striving to conceal, neg-

---

Note: This essay was originally appeared in German as 'Geschichtswissenschaft und gesellschaftliche Differenzierung: Überlegungen zur historischen Erforschung von Differenzierungsprozessen', in: Dilek Dizdar et al. (eds.), *Humandifferenzierung: Disziplinäre Perspektiven und empirische Sondierungen*, Weilerswist 2021, 35–57. I thank the publisher Velbrück Wissenschaft for permission to publish this translation. The translation was funded by the Deutsche Forschungsgemeinschaft (DFG, German Research Foundation) – Project-ID 442261292 – SFB 1482.

ate, bridge and overcome them.[1] Of particular interest here are the historical practices of differentiation and their scope.

Historical Theories of Differentiation and the Present Day

The various theories on past social differentiation are shaped by contemporary approaches, because even historians can never completely leave their own time behind. Conversely, the analysis of historical differentiation can lead to quite contradictory conclusions with regard to the present. Contemporary analyses and empirical investigations of the past therefore stand in an indissoluble interrelationship. As an introduction to the considerations on the historical research of differentiation processes, this problem will be exemplified by dealing with religious-confessional distinctions in the pre-modern era.[2] This is intended to illustrate by way of example how, against the background of functional differentiation, depending on the epochal focus of research, different conditions for the social treatment of difference come into view before or after the time around 1800, i.e. that epochal turning point which is regarded as the transition from a stratified to a functionally differentiated social order. The study of categories in the long run makes it possible to understand actualisations and superimpositions of historical categories of difference.

European societies in the early modern period knew various procedures for dealing with religious-confessional difference, which was one of the central distinctions that repeatedly led to fierce conflicts in numerous fields in the era from the European expansion and the Reformation to the French Revolution, and is also invoked again today, for example, in the Western confrontation with

---

[1] This overview has benefited from discussions at the Leibniz Institute of European History in the context of its research agenda "Negotiating Differences in Modern Europe" (see Leibniz-Institut für Europäische Geschichte (2018), *Umgang mit Differenz im Europa der Neuzeit: Ergebnisse und Impulse 2012–2017*, Mainz 2018; urn:nbn:de:0159–2018092704). Research on the subject is vast and cannot be comprehensively referenced in this article; references merely provide further reading.

[2] On pre-modernity as a concept Christian Jaser, Matthias Pohlig and Ute Lotz-Heumann (eds.), *Alteuropa – Vormoderne – Neue Zeit: Epochen und Dynamiken der europäischen Geschichte (1200–1800)*, Berlin 2012.

Islam:[3] first, there were attempts to legitimise the respective political-territorial rule with a certain truth of faith and to establish a religiously homogeneous subjecthood by marginalising dissenting positions and expelling their adherents or forcing them to convert. This form of dealing with confessional differences caused many groups to become religious refugees – from the Mudéjares on the Iberian Peninsula during the Reconquista and the expulsion of the Moors in 1609, to the Huguenots in the second half of the seventeenth century, to the Salzburg exiles of 1731.[4] Since complete homogeneity could not be achieved, the homogenisation measures also repeatedly led to dissimulation, to going underground or even to demonstrative martyrdom.

Secondly, religious conflict could be defused by differentiating between public and private religious practice, whereby the deviant, private religious practice was to remain invisible and its adherents were disadvantaged in political-public life.[5] Minorities paid for their religious toleration in the private sphere with special political loyalty to the authorities protecting them. This reveals an approach to social differentiation between religious and political order that was not self-evident in early modern Europe. Theological uncompromisingness, which did not want to distinguish between inner and outer creed, thereby strengthened the superiority of politics over religion by indirectly favouring the peace-making role of the rulers. Thirdly, there were peace agreements that guaranteed mutual religious freedom when there was a kind of balance of power between opposing confessional parties within a ruling structure. This religious freedom was usually a privilege of the estates, not an individual right. The institutions of the Holy Roman Empire, which existed until 1806, functioned according to parity rules: the constitution and the political bodies here were impregnated with confession-

---

[3] Barbara Stollberg-Rilinger, 'Unversöhnte Verschiedenheit', in: Johannes Paulmann, Matthias Schnettger and Thomas Weller (Eds.), *Unversöhnte Verschiedenheit: Verfahren zur Bewältigung religiös-konfessioneller Differenz in der europäischen Neuzeit*, Göttingen 2016, 197–203.

[4] In general, on refugees of faith Joachim Bahlcke, (ed.), *Glaubensflüchtlinge: Ursachen, Formen und Auswirkungen frühneuzeitlicher Konfessionsmigration in Europa*, Berlin 2008; on those mentioned here as examples Leonard P. Harvey, *Muslims in Spain: 1500 to 1614*, Chicago 2005; Mercedes García-Arenal and Gerard Wiegers, *Los moriscos – Expulsión y diaspora: Una perspectiva internacional*, Valencia 2016; Alexander Schunka, *Die Hugenotten: Geschichte, Religion, Kultur*, München 2019; Mack Walker, *Der Salzburger Handel: Vertreibung und Errettung der Salzburger Protestanten im 18. Jahrhundert*, Göttingen 1997.

[5] On the distinction between public, private and domestic religious practice around 1600, see Christopher Voigt-Goy, '"Öffentliche", "private" und "häusliche" Religionsausübung: Zur Herausbildung ihrer begrifflichen Unterscheidung um 1600', in: Henning P. Jürgens and Christian Volkmar Witt (eds.), *An den Rand gedrängt – den Rand gewählt: Marginalisierungsstrategien in der Frühen Neuzeit*, Leipzig 2021, 189–206.

al antagonisms, as it were. Since the confessional distinctions were not abolished but perpetuated in procedures, they could, however, also repeatedly lead to open conflicts.

A conceivable fourth variant, namely the religious neutrality of state institutions, was difficult to practise in the early modern period because rule was not sufficiently depersonalised. In the Old Empire, the principle cuius regio, eius religio of 1555 was not implemented everywhere, but could also lead to different forms of toleration of dissenting denominations within a ruling territory, especially in Protestant areas. In 1648, the Peace of Westphalia established practices in such a way that at least the Catholic, Lutheran and Reformed subjects no longer had to follow a change of confession by the prince. However, they were (still) classified according to their different confessions and religions and, if necessary, possessed different privileges.[6] In the European dominions, certain confessions enjoyed an almost exclusive monopoly under state law until the nineteenth century and partly beyond. Only later was state neutrality (not necessarily equal treatment, as the example of the so-called Free Churches in Germany shows) possible both towards the various major Christian denominations and towards members of the Jewish faith. This by no means excluded continued social discrimination and a return to state oppression up to expulsion and extermination.

From the analysis of these procedures, the early modern historian Barbara Stollberg-Rilinger concluded that religious diversity could only be "reconciled" to a limited extent in the early modern period because law, politics and religion were not sufficiently disentangled, i.e. the functional differentiation of society had not been completed. "Reconciled" diversity was only possible when potential disputes over religious differences could be settled "in formalised legal channels that were the same for all participants".[7] Legal equality and legal-secular procedures are thus achievements of modernity that make it possible to deal peacefully with religious differences. However, formal-legal decisiveness and unambiguity in dealing with religious difference and its political consequences can – according to my perspective from the observation of the last 200 years – at the same time solidify differences, reinforce them and dramatize small differences. This may lead to actions that deepen social and political antagonisms. It is there-

---

[6] On the development from the "Cuius regio, eius religio" principle to the tiered religious freedom of the Peace of Westphalia, see Horst Dreier, *Staat ohne Gott: Religion in der säkularen Moderne*, München 2018, 64–77; on subject rights Bernd Christian Schneider, *Ius reformandi: Die Entwicklung eines Staatskirchenrechts von seinen Anfängen bis zum Ende des Alten Reiches*, Tübingen 2001; for the European consolidation of confessional plurality Wayne te Brake, *Religious War and Religious Peace in Early Modern Europe*, Cambridge 2017, 280–316.

[7] Stollberg-Rilinger, 'Unversöhnte Verschiedenheit', 203.

fore necessary to create the political and social conditions not only for legally secured procedures in dealing with religious difference, but also for an individually and collectively acceptable ambiguity and dissimulation.[8] The call for tolerance in Sunday speeches is less effective for this than a staged difference in association with practised ambiguity, which veils differences to a certain extent without reconciling them and relies on more "tolerance of ambiguity" than can currently be practised.[9] For the twenty-first century, therefore, a look at the successful, but also the failed procedures and practices of the early modern period is quite instructive. In other words, learning from the early modern period means practising differentiation, not "reconciling" differences.

The two observations – the (lack of the) prerequisite of legal-secular procedures of decision-making in dealing with differences and the (continuing) necessity of practised ambiguity and indecision – do not contradict each other, but they show that depending on the respective epochal point of view, different phenomena come into view. Early modern research emphasises the late and gradual development of legal-secular procedures for dealing with religious difference, while a development towards the creation of unambiguity and a compulsion to confess becomes recognisable in the nineteenth and twentieth centuries. From this, more tolerance of ambiguity and corresponding patterns of behaviour can be demanded for the present – with reference to the practices of dissimulation in the early modern period. The conclusions based on historical findings, which in turn are based on the theory of functional differentiation of religion, politics and law, thus also raise questions about the historical background of social theoretical approaches. Which theories of differentiation are designed at certain times and why are they applied to the past or not, and when? Societies, past and present, can not only be analysed in terms of their functional, stratificational and socio-cultural differentiation, but the formation of theories itself takes place in historically specific contexts of differentiation. For the theorising of cultural human differentiation, i.e. meaningful differentiation, one can also ask

---

[8] Johannes Paulmann, 'Verfahren zur Bewältigung religiös-konfessioneller Differenz – eine gesellschaftliche und politische Herausforderung in der europäischen Neuzeit', in: Johannes Paulmann, Matthias Schnettger and Thomas Weller (eds.), *Unversöhnte Verschiedenheit: Verfahren zur Bewältigung religiös-konfessioneller Differenz in der europäischen Neuzeit*, Göttingen 2016, 9–17.

[9] Thomas Bauer, *Die Kultur der Ambiguität: Eine andere Geschichte des Islams*, Berlin 2011; Thomas Bauer, *Die Vereindeutigung der Welt: Über den Verlust an Mehrdeutigkeit und Vielfalt*, Ditzingen 2018; and Barbara Stollberg-Rilinger, 'Einleitung', in: Andreas Pietsch and Barbara Stollberg-Rilinger (eds.), *Konfessionelle Ambiguität: Uneindeutigkeit und Verstellung als religiöse Praxis in der Frühen Neuzeit*, Gütersloh 2013, 9–26.

why it is being advanced in the present in particular.[10] Is it the particular pressure of globalisation and individualisation in Western societies that stimulates the theorisation of the elementary process of differentiation between people? Is it the insight and experience of living in an ethnically and religiously diversified migration society? Or is it an awareness of advanced individuality with multiple possibilities of self-description? These questions are not intended as a normative orientation of social analysis, as tends to happen in the case of the intersectionality approach, but rather as an attempt to self-historicise theory-building, which can probably only be done in a really well-founded way by future historians. It should be pointed out that not only the study of the past, but also the analysis of the present is location-bound and thus historically situated. In the following, let us look, in detail, at the four different perspectives on historical forms of differentiation mentioned at the beginning.

Functional Differentiation – A Theory of (Pre-)Modernity

From a historical perspective, the theory of functional differentiation divides European history into pre-modern and modern times with the formation of individual, autonomous subsystems of politics, law, economics, science, religion, art, etc.[11] To the extent that these functional systems make certain demands on individuals, they have a socially differentiating effect on the one hand by differentiating people in their roles according to performance and professional competences (in politicians, judges, entrepreneurs, professors, pastors, artists, etc.). On the other hand, they include all members in their so-called audience roles (as voters, citizens, customers, students, believers, museum visitors, etc.). The theory offers a model for the analysis of European-Western societies, especially in the twentieth century. Unlike exclusion in class societies, for example, it emphasises the performance requirement and the roles of individuals, of which individuals must or can adopt or choose several depending on their life-historical or situational affiliation to a subsystem.

---

10 For an explanation of the loss or gain of meaning of distinctive categories and their reference since the 1960s to identity semantics in functionally differentiated society, the social visibility of categorical belonging and the global changes in categories of persons, Bettina Heintz, 'Kategoriale Ungleichheit und die Anerkennung von Differenz', in: Stefan Hirschauer (ed.), *Un/doing Differences: Praktiken der Humandifferenzierung*, Weilerswist 2017, 79–115.
11 Niklas Luhmann, *Die Gesellschaft der Gesellschaft*, Frankfurt / Main 1997, 707–776.

In historiography, functional differentiation, closely linked to modernisation theory, has been used to capture the epochal difference of modern societies since the period around the French Revolution compared to earlier eras.[12] However, the categorical division into early modern and late modern societies using functional differentiation needs to be looked at more closely. A general problem is that historians often accept functional differentiation as a template without examining the historical process more closely, thus reinforcing the segmentation of historiography by epoch.[13] One point of criticism is the assumption that contemporary societies are more complex than earlier ones. This is the impression that historians of later periods tend to give when they follow the theory of functional differentiation and their own more or less admitted ignorance. The above observations on the production of unambiguity through modern, legal-secular procedures and the importance of tolerance of ambiguity should add a question mark to this and point to the complexity of social differentiations in pre-modern Europe. Furthermore, it would be necessary to determine more precisely how the transition from pre-modern to modern, functionally differentiated society took place. The sociologist Niklas Luhmann already pointed out that the change was actually improbable[14], something that historians and social theorists alike forget when they assume a logical sequence. Where are the historical actors in this sociological grand theory, who were the actors of social change? This question is primarily directed at historians who describe comprehensive, long-term historical processes, because historical science usually tends to focus on the acting individuals and groups. The objection also comes from sociology itself.[15]

In principle, the scope of functional differentiation must be critically examined, not only where and how it came to bear in Europe (for example, in urban or rural societies), but also the extent to which this historical change was a European-Western one. Historians who have studied Europe's colonial and imperial

---

[12] Kevin Passmore, 'History and Social Science in the West', in: Axel Schneider and Daniel Woolf (eds.), *The Oxford History of Historical Writing, vol. 5: Historical Writing since 1945*, Oxford 2011, 199–219.

[13] The German concept of "historical social science", which focused on the nineteenth and twentieth centuries, had been strongly guided by modernization theory since the 1960s, while elsewhere internationally modernity critique was already stirring – see Georg G. Iggers, *Geschichtswissenschaft im 20. Jahrhundert: Ein kritischer Überblick im internationalen Zusammenhang*, Göttingen 2007, 65–74.

[14] Luhmann, *Gesellschaft*, 707.

[15] Uwe Schimank, *Differenzierung und Integration der modernen Gesellschaft: Beiträge zur akteurzentrierten Differenzierungstheorie 1*, Wiesbaden 2005; Uwe Schimank, *Teilsystemische Autonomie und politische Gesellschaftssteuerung: Beiträge zur akteurzentrierten Differenzierungstheorie 2*, Wiesbaden 2006.

relations with the "rest of the world" have long thought in terms of "expansion". Not only economic and political power relations played a role, but also cultural ones in terms of the concepts and theories with which foreign societies were understood by historical actors. Does Europe implicitly end for historians where no comparable functional differentiation can be observed, for example between religion and politics, and does Europe still end there today? In the meantime, there is a programmatic awareness of Eurocentrism in historical scholarship, so that historical "interconnections" are analysed in both directions and Europe is understood as a province in the world.[16] However, also in the sense of Dipesh Chakrabarty, it is important not to lose sight of the provincialisation through Europe, i.e. to take into account that European concepts and theories were carried into the "provinces" of the world and adopted there and adapted to the circumstances. With regard to functional differentiation, it would thus have to be examined to what extent it is a Eurocentric theory that thinks of world society but assumes that social processes take place in the same way everywhere. Is this assumption appropriate for a historical understanding of non-European societies and for the development of a world society?[17] This question is addressed to historians as well as social theorists.

If we start historically from functional differentiation, then the question arises in the present whether it is still the predominant form of the major social divisions.[18] Are there not other prevailing principles of differentiation developing as a result of the change in electronic communication, such as the different position in networks that determine social life and action and which increasingly span the functional subsystems? More pointedly: are we perhaps in parts approaching again personal forms of differentiation of the early modern period?[19] When and why did the boundaries between the subsystems begin to dissolve? Turned differently once again: what was actually the contemporary background for the theory of functional differentiation? We should also historicise this theory

---

16 Sebastian Conrad, Shalini Randeria and Regina (eds.), *Jenseits des Eurozentrismus: Postkoloniale Perspektiven in den Geschichts- und Kulturwissenschaften*. Frankfurt / Main 2013; and Jens Adam, Regina Römhild et al. (eds.), *Europa dezentrieren: Globale Verflechtungen neu denken*, Frankfurt / Main 2019.
17 Cf. Bernhard Gißibl and Isabella Löhr (eds.), *Bessere Welten: Kosmopolitismus in den Geschichtswissenschaften*. Frankfurt / Main 2017.
18 Dirk Baecker, *Studien zur nächsten Gesellschaft*, Frankfurt / Main 2007.
19 With regard to patronage, see Birgit Emich, 'Normen an der Kreuzung: Intersektionalität statt Konkurrenz oder: Die unaufhebbare Gleichzeitigkeit von Amt, Stand und Patronage', in: Arne Kasten and Hillard von Thiessen (eds.), *Normenkonkurrenz in historischer Perspektive*, Berlin 2015, 83–100.

formation and ask how it was embedded in the contemporary historical context of the Cold War and the upheaval of the 1970s.

Stratificational Differentiation – A Theory of Social (In)Equality

The second approach to exploring social distinctions historically is stratificational differentiation. This is a form of hierarchical differentiation that determines the place of persons in society as "above" / "below" or "further up" / "further down", but also as "central" and "peripheral". The focus of interest in historical research from a stratificational perspective is on social inequalities. Here, historical scholarship has dealt intensively with early modern estate-based society and the class society of the nineteenth and twentieth centuries. Both forms of stratification are dynamic, for contrary to the statics repeatedly assumed from the perspective of the late modern period, the estate-based society was also markedly mobile.[20] In terms of social mobility, it was above all the university, the clergy, the state administration, the military and trading companies that offered opportunities for advancement.

It is worthwhile to systematically ask the other way round, i.e. to look at statics in the late modern period, i.e. to doubt the self-evident assumption of its peculiar dynamics, and not only with regard to the preservation of the political-social power of elites. A starting thesis with regard to social inequality is that in the framework of estate-based society, social advancement (i.e. overcoming unequal conditions) was possible but required legitimisation, while in the subsequent social order, insofar as an ideal of equality or equality of opportunity had prevailed, persisting inequality required explanation. Thinking further and politically, a tension arises between equality and participation[21], because equality can have an anti-plural effect, but at the same time allows for the democratic participation of those who are equal in principle. Conversely, inequality ensures plurality, but limits participation to a select elite.

Several key categories have been identified in historical research on social inequality. As a fundamental distinction in estate-based society, "the social position of individuals and groups and their access to social resources in estates

---

20 Winfried Schulze (ed.), *Ständische Gesellschaft und soziale Mobilität*, München 1988.
21 Lars Behrisch, 'Vormoderne Wurzeln der Demokratie – und ihr politisches Erklärungspotential', in: *Geschichte für heute* 11/2 (2018), 36-47; cf. Dan Diner, *Das Jahrhundert verstehen: Eine universalhistorische Deutung*. Frankfurt / Main 2000, 46–47, 65–67.

society was very much based on the respective degree of social prestige or 'honour' ascribed to a person or group of persons by their social environment."[22] Honour did allow for a gradual distinction, not only a binary one between honourable and dishonourable. In the Ancien Régime, social order and hierarchies were made visible and affirmed in particular by means of symbolic communication.[23] Conflicts of rank and precedent are therefore regarded as a further structural feature of estate-based society. An essential part of its internal dynamics stemmed from the recurrent struggles for distinction between different social groups. Another key category of differentiation was "potestas", i.e. the legitimate participation in ruling power. It has also been seen as a "dominant" early modern fundamental category.[24] Religion and confession, which have already been mentioned at the beginning, should be added.[25] How does it now relate to social inequality, to the different degree of honour, participation in ruling power or religious affiliation in the later modern period? It is well known that honour played an important role in the nineteenth century, although not one that comprehensively structured social relations, but gender distinctions.[26] Denominational distinctions shaped societies from the culture wars of the nineteenth century until well into the twentieth century, while religious affiliation has once again become a socio-political category of difference in recent decades.

Asked further, are there similarly central distinctions for the social positioning of individuals in the later modern period? What social differentiations would we call structural features? If we consider the disposal of economic resources and access to markets as the basis for capitalist class society, after the earlier de-

---

22 Marian Füssel and Thomas Weller (eds.), *Soziale Ungleichheit und ständische Gesellschaft: Theorien und Debatten in der Frühneuzeitforschung*, Frankfurt / Main 2011, 6, 10; Sybille Backmann et al. (eds.), *Ehrkonzepte in der Frühen Neuzeit: Identitäten und Abgrenzungen*, Berlin 1998.
23 Barbara Stollberg-Rilinger, *Des Kaisers alte Kleider: Verfassungsgeschichte und Symbolsprache des Alten Reiches*, München 2008; Barbara Stollberg-Rilinger, *Rituale*, Frankfurt / Main 2019.
24 Michaela Hohkamp, 'Im Gestrüpp der Kategorien: Zum Gebrauch von "Geschlecht" in der Frühen Neuzeit', in: Andrea Griesebner / Christina Lutter (eds.), *Die Macht der Kategorien*, Innsbruck 2002, 6–17.
25 Matthias Bähr, Florian Kühnel (eds.), *Verschränkte Ungleichheit: Praktiken der Intersektionalität in der Frühen Neuzeit*, Berlin 2018, 20–21; Falko Schnicke, 'Terminologie, Erkenntnisinteresse, Methode und Kategorien: Grundfragen intersektionaler Forschung', in: Christian Klein and Falko Schnicke (eds.), *Intersektionalität und Narratologie: Methoden – Konzepte – Analysen*, Trier 2014, 1–32.
26 Ute Frevert, *Ehrenmänner: Das Duell in der bürgerlichen Gesellschaft*, München 1991; Johannes Paulmann, *Pomp und Politik: Monarchenbegegnungen in Europa zwischen Ancien Régime und Erstem Weltkrieg*, Paderborn 2000, 102–104, 171–173.

bates on class(es), class position and class consciousness[27], a current proposal would be to systematically examine 'achievement and performance' as a central measure historically.[28] How was achievement formed, cultivated or restored? What systems of order (school, companies, sports competitions, etc.) for performance emerged? Which individual or group-related differentiations according to achievements had a socially integrating or excluding effect? In which contexts and when did performance lose or lose its structure-forming character? This brings us back to the present: are there still any central standards for social differentiation today? Or have they lost their orientation value through processes of individualisation, pluralisation, self-dramatization and digitalisation?

Socio-Cultural Differentiation – A Theory of Identity Construction

A third approach to exploring social distinctions historically is socio-cultural differentiation through affiliation and group formation. It is based on a form of differentiation that determines the affiliation of persons to collectives through the assumption and production of similarity and the non-affiliation through the construction of otherness or deviation. Sociologically speaking, it is thus about membership, i.e. the characteristics of people that are shared with others and make them exemplars of social entities (especially collectives).[29] In historiography, the concept of identity associated with collective membership has been critically reflected upon.[30] Identity is understood in historiography as a practice of identification, not as an analytically or historically predetermined category.

As alternative analytical terms to "identity", the sociologist Rogers Brubaker and the historian Frederick Cooper use firstly identification and categorisation, with which processes of status ascription can be investigated; secondly self-understanding and social location, in order to capture situational subjectivity; fi-

---

27 Georg G. Iggers, *Geschichtswissenschaft im 20. Jahrhundert: Ein kritischer Überblick im internationalen Zusammenhang*, Göttingen 2007, 70–73, 80–86; Jürgen Kocka, *Weder Stand noch Klasse: Unterschichten um 1800*, Bonn 1990.
28 Nina Verheyen, *Die Erfindung der Leistung*, München 2018.
29 Stefan Hirschauer, 'Un/doing Differences: Die Kontingenz sozialer Zugehörigkeiten', in: *Zeitschrift für Soziologie* 43 (2014), 170–191; Stefan Hirschauer, 'Menschen unterscheiden: Grundlinien einer Theorie der Humandifferenzierung', in: *Zeitschrift für Soziologie* 50 (2021), 155–174.
30 Lutz Niethammer, *Kollektive Identität: Heimliche Quellen einer unheimlichen Konjunktur*, Reinbek 2000.

nally thirdly commonality, connectedness and groupness, with which communitarisation and the subjective sense of belonging are to be captured.[31] In the historical analysis of identification practices, the focus is on the actors and the processes; internal differentiations, different forms of expression and characteristics of identity are considered from the outset. A distinction can also be made between self-identification and the identification by others when identity and status are ascribed through signs or papers and the ordering structures attached to them. The practices were also an element of relational claims in the process of cultural sovereignty politics in the sense of self-assertion and the claim to interpreting one's social group.[32]

Belonging as another central concept that has become common in historical scholarship to study social (group) differentiation puts a special emphasis on the perception and practices of the actors as well as their relations to each other.[33] Belonging is understood as "an emotionally charged social location that emerges through the interplay of (1) perceptions and performances of commonality, (2) social relations of reciprocity, and (3) material and immaterial connections or attachments".[34] Belonging, defined here in sociological terms, forms an essential part of collective identity constructions for descriptions of difference. Historical forms of the formation of societies were, for example, families, clans, clientele and patronage systems, brotherhoods, friendships, networks, compatriots, associations, etc. In historical research, several research perspectives have been pursued in this context: identity and alterity research;[35] postcolonial hybridity;[36]

---

[31] Rogers Brubaker and Frederick Cooper, 'Beyond "identity"', in: *Theory and Society* 29 (2000), 1–47.
[32] Gregor Feindt, Bernhard Gißibl and Johannes Paulmann (eds.), *Kulturelle Souveränität: Politische Deutungs- und Handlungsmacht jenseits des Staates im 20. Jahrhundert*, Göttingen 2017; Gregor Feindt, Bernhard Gissibl and Johannes Paulmann, 'Introduction: Cultural sovereignty – claims, forms and contexts beyond the modern state', in: European History Yearbook 21 (2020), 1–20.
[33] Stefan Hirschauer, 'Humandifferenzierung: Modi und Grade sozialer Zugehörigkeit', in: Hirschauer, *Un/doing Differences*, Weilerswist 2017, 29–54.
[34] Joanna Pfaff-Czarneka, *Zugehörigkeit in der mobilen Welt: Politiken der Verortung*, Göttingen 2012, 12; emphasis added.
[35] Among others, Moniak Fludernik, Hans-Joachim Gehrke (eds.), *Grenzgänger zwischen Kulturen*, Würzburg 1999; Monika Fludernik, Hans-Joachim Gehrke, (eds.), *Identitäten und Alteritäten: Normen, Ausgrenzungen, Hybridisierungen und "Acts of Identity"*, Würzburg 2004.
[36] Hybridity as a postcolonial concept propagates a different understanding than identity practices. It serves as a guiding term to describe cultural mixes and mixtures and as a positive counter-concept to notions of cultural purity. Hybridity is also demarcated from the conceptualization of multiculturalism, which with its central categories of integration, acculturation or assimilation tends to suggest a multiplicity of separable cultures. The concept of hybridity does not em-

pluralisation and authority[37], thus also in a European and global historical perspective the study of processes of marginalisation.[38]

More generally, a relational perspective has been put forward on the history of society: the focus here is on social differentiations that are first constituted and constructed through relationships between individuals and groups of people.[39] The study of socio-cultural group formation tends to make differences smaller because it focuses on belonging through similarity rather than exclusion through deviation. Although group formation can be studied across epochs, it would also be necessary to ask about epoch-specificity and epoch-spanning commonalities: how strong were social attachments and bonds? Is it possible to work with identification and self-image equally in all societies or would it not be necessary to take into account the historical development and changeability of the idea of individuality and thus the social constitution of the individual as part of a historical process?[40]

---

phasize cultural diversity and its possibility, but cultural difference and its conditions of articulation. Two varieties of hybridity can be distinguished in the cultural-scientific-political debate: a critical-emancipatory understanding of hybridity as a strategy and possibility of subaltern articulation of difference, subversive appropriation and amalgamation as well as the critical questioning of asymmetries and binary oppositions; and a liberal-permissive understanding of hybridity as an appreciative valorization of marginality and mixing, which is increasingly capitalistically and politically exploited as a productive factor; see Feindt, Gißibl and Paulmann, *Kulturelle Souveränität*, 29–30.

37 Wulf Oesterreicher, Gerhard Regn and Winfried Schulze (eds.), *Autorität der Form – Autorisierung – Institutionelle Autorität*, Münster 2003; Andreas Höfele, Jan-Dirk Müller and Wulf Oesterreicher (eds.), *Die Frühe Neuzeit: Revisionen einer Epoche*, Berlin 2013.

38 Christof Dejung and Martin Lengwiler (eds.), *Ränder der Moderne: Neue Perspektiven auf die Europäische Geschichte (1800–1930)*, Köln 2016.

39 Marian Füssel, 'Die relationale Gesellschaft: Zur Konstitution ständischer Ordnung in der Frühen Neuzeit aus praxeologischer Perspektive', in: Dagmar Freist (ed.), *Diskurse – Körper – Artefakte: Historische Praxeologie in der Frühneuzeitforschung*, Bielefeld 2015, 115–137; Angelika Epple, 'Relationale Geschichtsschreibung: Gegenstand, Erkenntnisinteresse und Methode globaler und weltregionaler Geschichtsschreibung', in: *H-Soz-Kult*, 02.11.2017, <www.hsozkult.de/debate/id/diskussionen-4291> (2020–08–02); Anne Friedrichs, 'Placing Migration in Perspective: Neue Wege einer relationalen Geschichtsschreibung', in: *Geschichte und Gesellschaft* 44/2 (2018), 167–195.

40 For criticism of the idea that the (Western) individual is the main point of reference for historical processes, see Hans Medick, '"Missionare im Ruderboot"? Ethnologische Erkenntnisinteressen als Herausforderung an die Sozialgeschichte', in: *Geschichte und Gesellschaft*, 10/3 (1984), 295–319, here 318, with reference to Geertz; more recent historical research takes a critical view of the thesis of the discovery of the individual in the Renaissance, see Valentin Groebner, *Der Schein der Person: Steckbrief, Ausweis und Kontrolle im Europa des Mittelalters*, München

Intersectionality as Historicization of Conjunctures of Social Inequality

The concept of intersectionality has also been taken up in historical studies and, contrary to its originally static approach[41], has been modified in such a way that contingent conjunctures of difference come into view. In the cultural and social sciences, intersectionality has been used above all in gender studies, in studies on racism/ethnicity, but also in studies that focus on religious or confessional categories (such as Jewish studies or Protestantism or Catholicism studies); it also plays a certain role for area studies, insofar as a certain space is thought of as a special one "according to its character". These various studies focus on a certain category of difference, which they regard as dominant. They are often interdisciplinary in orientation, so that the historical perspective only provides one of several on the development, effect and, in many cases, politically demand for overcoming the category under study. The respective determining category of difference is usually seen as discriminatory or as producing inequality. Historical research on intersectionality also tends to see the respective category as effective across epochs, but in terms of historical semantics it does take into account the historical change of the category assumed to be decisive.[42] Historians also generally recognise, in the sense of the intersectionality approach, that usually not only one particular category of difference played a role in the formation of social groups and stratification as well as in the actions of individuals. Which attributed characteristic was salient, they determine temporally and spatially context-dependent.

While a rather simple understanding focuses on the addition of several, fixed categories of distinction that restrict access to social resources of certain groups[43], historians have tried to develop the concept further – while retaining the term – by looking at the contingency and conjunctures in the interaction

---

2004, and Annette Vowinckel, *Das Relationale Zeitalter: Individualität, Normalität und Mittelmaß in der Kultur der Renaissance*. Paderborn 2011, 7–15 and 26–38.

41 Kimberlé Crenshaw, 'Mapping the Margins: Intersectionality, Identity Politics, and Violence Against Women of Color', in: *Stanford Law Review* 43 (1994), 1241–1299.

42 For example, Francisco Bethencourt, *Racisms: From the Crusades to the Twentieth Century*, Princeton 2014.

43 Kerstin Palm, 'Einführung in das Konzept der Intersektionalität', in: Matthias Bähr and Florian Kühnel (eds.), *Ungleichheit: Praktiken der Intersektionalität in der Frühen Neuzeit*, Berlin 2018, 39–53; Falko Schnicke, 'Terminologie, Erkenntnisinteresse, Methode und Kategorien: Grundfragen intersektionaler Forschung', in: Klein and Schnicke, *Intersektionalität und Narratologie*, Trier 2014, 1–32.

of categories of difference. Accordingly, intersectionality should not only be understood as multiple disadvantages, but also as an interplay, but also counter-interplay of several categories of difference. In this way, firstly, processes of differentiation in the sense of the production of diversity (not only inequalities) can be analysed, and secondly, privilege (and not only marginalisation) can also be analysed through the interaction of several categories and the connection of the privileging of one with the marginalisation of the other. Thirdly, this allows above all to look at different levels: the micro-level of the (everyday) interaction of historical actors, the level of socio-political structures (decision-making instances, infrastructures, norm systems) and finally also the level of perceptions, ideas and representations. This brings historically specific constellations into the focus of the study. Fourthly, it will be asked historically how the weight of certain categories changed in the medium or long term, how leading categories asserted themselves and which former distinctions were pushed to the margins, so to speak. In this way, historical conjunctures become recognisable, both in the sense of ups and downs and in the sense of an interaction of contingent categories of difference. Finally and fifthly, category formation can be understood historically, i.e. the categories themselves cannot be understood as given, but they can be seen as the interplay of different distinctions on different levels – as becoming, solidifying or also dissolving. Historical processes of (de-) differentiation thus come into focus.

These recent reflections on historical intersectionality have moved significantly away from the concept of intersectionality, which is the intersection of forms of social inequality that are defined in advance in terms of structural theory. They come very close to the concept of human differentiation and, among other things, also refer directly to the approach of undoing gender by Stefan Hirschauer.[44] It is remarkable that historians are writing here who deal with the early modern period, i.e. the three centuries before 1800 and the so-called pre-modern period.[45] The categorical separation of the epochs, which is based

---

[44] Bähr and Kühnel, 'Verschränkte Ungleichheit', 26.
[45] See also more generally Vera Kallenberg, '"Intersektionalität" als "Histoire croisée": Zum Verhältnis von "Intersektionalität", Geschlechterforschung und Geschichtswissenschaften', in: Marita Günther-Saeed and Esther Hornung (eds.), *Zwischenbestimmungen: Identität und Geschlecht jenseits der Fixierbarkeit?*, Würzburg 2012, 75–118, and, in the context of migration history studies, Vera Kallenberg, '"und würde auch sonst gesehen haben, wie sie sich durchbrächte": Migration und Intersektionalität in Frankfurter Kriminalakten über jüdische Dienstmägde um 1800', in: Edeltraud Aubele and Gabriele Pieri (eds.), *Femina migrans: Frauen in Migrationsprozessen (18.–20. Jahrhundert)*, Sulzbach 2011, 39–67; and Malou Schrover, Deirdre Moloney (eds.), *Gender, Migration and Categorisation: Making Distinctions between Migrants in Western Countries, 1945–2010*, Amsterdam 2013.

on the theory of functional differentiation, seems to make little sense, if not hinder historical investigations of human differentiation and the question of how people differ from one another.

Historical Anthropology – A Methodological Approach to Socialisation through (De)Differentiation

A "history of differences" is a history of the modern era from the perspective of how people distinguished themselves from one another by linguistically naming and performatively marking differences from others, by establishing them through rules and trying to preserve them in procedures or institutionally, or by striving to disguise, negate, bridge and overcome distinctions. Historical anthropology offers a useful approach to the history of differences. It makes it possible to link up with current developments in the social and cultural sciences and can be well combined with social and socio-theoretical questions of human differentiation. Historical anthropology is an approach to social and cultural history that became established in German historiography in the late 1970s. The historians who advanced it programmatically and empirically distinguished it from the paradigm of historical social science. They did not want to follow the "centrist and unilinear historical view", which classified social phenomena according to their position in the centre or on the margins of events within the framework of the great processes of modernisation, industrialisation and the construction of bureaucratic institutional and nation states.[46] Such a perspective, inspired by social science, dichotomously contrasted the subjective and objective dimensions and emphasised the efficacy of structures and historical processes compared to the agency and stubbornness of individuals. Those who took a historical anthropological approach, on the other hand, strove to explore the interrelationship of experiences and perceptions with the conditions of life, production and domination. Historical anthropology therefore emphasises the ongoing, cultural production of structures, contexts of action and social self-understanding. These were thus both a changeable, temporally and spatially specific component and at the same time a result of the behaviour, perception and experience of specific persons and groups of persons.[47]

---

[46] Medick, 'Missionare', 301–302.
[47] Ibid., 295–297.

The subject of historical-anthropological research interests were initially the supposed "losers" and the marginal phenomena of modernisation, such as the groups and strata that were pauperised in the course of the secular upheavals, furthermore popular cultural expressions and ways of thinking, or the history of women.[48] Encounters with "Foreigners" outside of Europe were also studied, but initially primarily those considered "foreign" in European history. A clear epochal focus was on the early modern period, the study of which subsequently provided essential impulses for a renewal and the development of what appeared to be worth knowing and relevant in history. Research interests expanded over the years.[49] Approaches to the history of the body and gender, the study of everyday, "little lives" and the analysis of self-testimonies and visual and media worlds remained important. In addition, there were areas such as the history of violence, economic history, the history of knowledge, global history or the history of material culture.[50]

Historical anthropology, as it has established itself in Germany strongly inspired above all by English-language social and cultural anthropology, can be understood as a history of culture, in the sense of culture as a practice of life, not as a delimited field of action. In the programmatic postulate of the historian Hans Medick in 1984, the interpretation of symbolic forms and their social and political use – inspired by Clifford Geertz – played a major role. Symbolic forms were supposed to overcome the problem of the inaccessibility of the "foreign", i.e. past subjective experiences, because the traditional hermeneutic procedure of historical work presupposed a cultural unity and the continuity of the context of experience, which, however, were no longer considered a given. As important as the semiotic decoding of diverse and hierarchical structures of meaning continues to be for historical-anthropological research, a praxeological tendency can be observed: interest is increasingly directed towards historical practices, patterns of action, behaviours and routines through which material resources and social relations were mobilised and thus options for action opened up.[51]

---

48 Ibid., 300–303.
49 Peter Burschel, 'Wie Menschen möglich sind: 20 Jahrgänge "Historische Anthropologie"', in: *Historische Anthropologie* 20/2 (2012), 152–161.
50 In addition to the essay by Medick, 'Missionare', widely cited in German research, Rebekka Habermas, Nils Minkmar (eds.), *Das Schwein des Häuptlings: Sechs Aufsätze zur Historischen Anthropologie*, Berlin 1992. The establishment of historical anthropology took place and became apparent in the journal *Historische Anthropologie: Kultur – Gesellschaft – Alltag*, published since 1993.
51 Burschel, 'Menschen', 159; Dagmar Freist (ed.), *Diskurse – Körper – Artefakte: Historische Praxeologie in der Frühneuzeitforschung*, Bielefeld 2015.

The starting point is thus no longer social groups or subjects, but rather housekeeping, consuming, arguing or even differentiating.[52]

In historical anthropology, as it is understood here, the focus is only ostensibly on "the human being", because its questions are by no means directed at the "essence of the human being" or elementary, biology-related and at the same time universally widespread behaviours such as birth, nutrition, reproduction, fighting and dying.[53] Rather, they aim at "historically changing forms of knowledge of and about human beings".[54] In other words, it is about the historically evolved and changeable plurality of people. Attention is focused on the question of "how people socialise and in doing so produce the symbolically mediated social that shapes them, but to which they can never be reduced".[55] Accordingly, the central problem is "how people in different social contexts and media constellations enter into a reflexive self-relationship that enables them to understand themselves in a specific way as acting, thinking and feeling subjects and to 'reinvent' themselves again and again." Jakob Tanner here highlights three thematic areas that are addressed in historical anthropology: first, the forms and media of human self-descriptions as well as the change of images of human beings;[56] second, social practices, communicative patterns of interaction as well as the symbolic forms and power relations that structure and regulate the social; third, the historicity of what is considered human nature.

Historical anthropology is close to a sociological approach such as human differentiation. Both choose a decidedly cultural approach to the analysis of societies. They explore symbolic forms and their social and political use; they distinguish different levels (or layers of meaning) from situational practices, through consolidation in intersubjective identifications and descriptions of belonging, to the symbolic designs of order in societies. Since the 2000s, historical-anthropological research has also examined distinction practices in estates-based society[57], highlighting the inner dynamics of estates-based society

---

52 Füssel, 'Relationale Gesellschaft', 136.
53 Clear demarcation from an ontological anthropology already in Medick, 'Missionare', 299–300.
54 Jakob Tanner, 'Historische Anthropologie', *Docupedia-Zeitgeschichte* [2012] DOI: http://dx.doi.org/10.14765/zzf.dok.2.278.v1 [2020–08–09].
55 Ibid., and the following quote.
56 For example, Katharina Stornig and Judith Becker 'Menschbilder in Missionszeitschriften: Ordnungen von Vielfalt um 1900', in: Judith Becker and Katharina Stornig (eds.), *Menschen – Bilder – Eine Welt: Ordnungen von Vielfalt in der religiösen Publizistik um 1900*, Göttingen 2018, 9–32.
57 Marian Füssel and Thomas Weller (eds.), *Ordnung und Distinktion: Praktiken sozialer Repräsentation in der ständischen Gesellschaft*, Münster 2005; Horst Carl and Patrick Schmidt (eds.),

through permanent differentiation. As a rule, the disputes over distinctions did not have the effect of overthrowing order, but were led by the effort to determine the respective place in the existing categories and classifications.

Finally, the historical-anthropological approach has recently been expanded in the sense of a global microhistory.[58] This has raised in a renewed form, on the one hand, the question of the synchronic and diachronic scope of ideas and practices and, on the other, the problem of the relations between different levels of investigation. In contrast to the German debates between everyday life and social history in the 1980s and 1990s, in which micro- and macro-history, agency and structure, and state description and processes of change were juxtaposed, the interaction, perspectives and selection of the different levels are now critically reflected upon, including their construction by researchers.[59] The levels range from subjective, situational and local perceptions, experiences and practices, their consolidation and institutionalisation in systems of norms and instances of control, to the infrastructures and conditions of possibility that may be formed globally.[60] Investigating how micro-, meso- and macro-forms interacted poses not only considerable analytical but also narrative challenges for historians. They also force us to think about the scope of contemporary categories and practices: in spatial terms, about the boundaries of European ways of thinking and behaving; in temporal terms, about the different speeds of their change and the resulting conflicts.[61] The questions about levels and ranges that are currently being raised in global microhistory relate to general problems of historiography. They refer to the concrete contexts and constellations that historians are interested in and in which people, even when they make distinctions, act, produce, confirm or modify through practices and form a social self-understanding. The study of human differentiation gains from this perspective by not only recognising the

---

Stadtgemeinde und Ständegesellschaft: Integration und Distinktion in der frühneuzeitlichen Stadt, Berlin 2007.
58 Francesca Trivellato, 'Is There a Future for Italian Microhistory in the Age of Global History?', in: *California Italian Studies* 2/1 (2011), http://escholarship.org/uc/item/0z94n9hq; Hans Medick, 'Turning Global: Microhistory in Extension', in: *Historische Anthropologie* 24/2 (2016), 241–252; Ian Gwinn, 'Going back to go forward? A reply to Hans Medick', *Historische Anthropologie* 24/3 (2016), 418–431; Giovanni Levi, 'Globale Mikrogeschichte als "Renaissance"? Ein Kommentar zu Hans Medick', in: *Historische Anthropologie* 25/1 (2017), 115–119.
59 Kallenberg, 'Intersektionalität', 98–101; Jan de Vries, 'Playing with Scales: The Global and the Micro, the Macro and the Nano', in: John-Paul A. Ghobrial (ed.), *Global History and Microhistory*, Oxford 2019, 23–36.
60 Romain Bertrand and Guillaume Calafat, 'La microhistoire globale: Affaire(s) à suivre', in: *Annales HSS* 73/1 (2018), 3–18.
61 Ibid.

persistence or disappearance of historical differentiations, but also by reflecting on the transformation of contemporary differentiations into history.

The anthropologically inspired analysis of historically changeable socialisation through (de)differentiations could represent an epochally and spatially open approach that, on the one hand, does not prescribe or presuppose a narrative for the history of social differentiation, but rather develops it. From the standpoint of the present, the result is a contradictory and multi-layered history of differentiation that reaches back into the pre-modern era in numerous references. On the other hand, such an approach allows a context-sensitive approach that reveals historical and contemporary constellations and conjunctures. It would be open to European and non-European studies as well as the relations between or the development of this historical-spatial distinction. Finally, such historical research would be suitable for taking up questions, methods and theoretical building blocks from other disciplines and also passing them on to them.

Biographical Notes

Noëmie Duhaut is a research associate at the Leibniz Institute of European History (IEG) Mainz. She received her PhD from University College London and previously held fellowships from the Arts and Humanities Research Council, the Posen Foundation, the German Historical Institute in Paris, the Hebrew University of Jerusalem, the Central European University in Budapest, and Dartmouth College. She was a guest professor at the University of Graz and is currently a fellow at the Herbert D. Katz Center for Advanced Judaic Studies at the University of Pennsylvania. She is completing a book manuscript on Jewish internationalism in the context of post-Ottoman state-building in the Balkans and writing a biography of the French Jewish politician Adolphe Crémieux. Recent publications include: '"A French Jew Emancipated the Blacks": Discursive Strategies of French Jews in the Age of Transnational Emancipations', in: *French Historical Studies* 44, no. 4, 2021, 645–674, https://doi.org/10.1215/00161071-9248713; 'L'Alliance israélite universelle, les Juifs roumains et l'idée d'Europe', in: *Archives Juives* 53, no. 2, 2020, 72–89, https://doi.org/10.3917/aj1.532.0072

Richard Herzog is a postdoctoral research fellow at the History Department of the Philipps-Universität Marburg and at the DFG Collaborative Research Centre/Transregio 138 "Dynamics of Security. Types of Securitization From a Historical Perspective". His research interests include Spanish America in a global perspective, Nahua history, as well as decolonial and transcultural studies. He has published on these topics, key publications are: 'Conferring a Universal Scope to Nahua Political Concepts: An aim in the works of Domingo de Chimalpahin (early 17th Century)', in: Laura Dierksmeier, Fabian Fechner, Kazuhisa Takeda (eds.): *Indigenous Knowledge as a Resource? Transmission, Reception, and Interaction of Global and Local Knowledge between Europe and the Americas, 1492–1800*, Tübingen 2021; 'Acolhua Past and Novohispanic Merit: Self and Community in Fernando de Alva Ixtlilxochitl's Struggles for a Cacicazgo', in: Nikolaus Böttcher, Stefan Rinke, Nino Vallen (eds.): *Distributive Struggle and the Self in the Early Modern Iberian World*, Stuttgart 2019.

Samuel B. Keeley is a postdoctoral fellow at the *Forschungszentrum Europa* at the University of Trier and an affiliated scholar at the Leibniz Institute of European History (IEG) Mainz. He completed his doctoral degree at the University of California, Los Angeles (UCLA) in 2019. He is currently working on completing a monograph entitled, "Awakening: Transnational Evangelicalism, Diplomacy, and Piety in the Anglo-German World: 1815–1871".

Riley Linebaugh is a research associate at the Leibniz Institute of European History (IEG) Mainz. Her current research examines the influence of African students in European universities during the period of decolonization. She completed her PhD, "Curating the Past: Britain's 'Migrated Archives' and the Struggle for Kenyan History", at Justus Liebig University. Previously, she obtained an M.A. in Archives and Records Management from University College London and worked professionally as an archivist in Uganda, England and the U.S. Her research interests include archival politics, colonial and imperial histories, and East Africa. Her recent publications include, together with James Lowry, 'The Archival Colour Line: Race, Records and Post-Colonial Custody', in: *Archives and Records* 42, no. 3, 2021, 1–20, DOI: 10.1080/23257962.2021.1940898; 'Coloniality and Power in Uganda's Archives', with Katherine Bruce-Lockhart, in: Katherine Bruce-Lockhart, Jon Earle, Nakanyike Musisi, Edgar Taylor (eds.), *Decolonisation and Public Life in Uganda* (James Currey, forthcoming).

Tom Menger is a postdoctoral research fellow at Ludwig-Maximilian University Munich. He defended his doctoral thesis entitled "The Colonial Way of War: Extreme Violence in Knowledge and Practice of Colonial Warfare in the British, German and Dutch Colonial Empires, c. 1890–1914" in 2021 at the University of Cologne. His research interests include colonial violence and war, transimperial history and the history of imperial infrastructure and oil exploration. He is the author of '"Press the Thumb onto the Eye": Moral Effect, Extreme Violence, and the Transimperial Notions of British, German and Dutch Colonial Warfare, c. 1890–1914', *Itinerario* 46, no. 1, 2022, 84–108, https://doi.org/10.1017/S0165115321000371. His article 'Concealing Colonial Comparability: British Exceptionalism, Imperial Violence, and the Dynamiting of Cave Refuges in Southern Africa, 1879–1897' has been accepted for publication with the *Journal of Imperial and Commonwealth History*.

Sara Müller has been a research assistant at the Department of Modern History at the University of Göttingen since October 2018. Her PhD project is part of the joint research project "Provenance Research on Non-European Collections and Ethnology in Lower Saxony" (PAESE). She works closely with the ethnographic collection at the University of Göttingen to research the provenance of objects from Oceania that were collected during German colonialism. Her research focuses on German colonial history in Oceania, the history of ethnographic collections and provenance research. She is currently working on the article 'Auf der Suche nach einer Win-Win-Situation', in: *Historische Anthropologie* 1 (2022). She is also the author of 'Ein Vermittler deutscher Kolonialgeschichte. Der Göttinger Kasuar-Dolch vom Sepik in Papua-Neuguinea', in: Ernst Seidl, Frank Steinheimer, Cornelia Weber (eds.): *Eine Frage der Perspektive. Objekte als Vermittler von Wissenschaft. Beiträge zum Workshop des Zentralmagazins Naturwissenschaftlicher Sammlungen (ZNS) der MLU Halle-Wittenberg.* Halle, 14.–15. Oktober 2020, Martin-Luther-Universität Halle-Wittenberg. Berlin 2021, edoc.hu-berlin.de/junges_forum (2022–01–24); 'Spoons are everything!', in: *'Wie Wissen Ausstellen' Blog des Forschungskollegs 'Wissen I Ausstellen'*, http://wie-wissen-ausstellen.uni-goettingen.de/2020/08/12/spoons-are-everything/ (2021–09–22).

Johannes Paulmann is Director of the Leibniz Institute of European History (IEG) Mainz and Professor of Modern History at Johannes Gutenberg-Universität Mainz. He was a distinguished visiting professor at the London School of Economics, St Antony's College Oxford and Sorbonne University Paris. His research interests cover the history of Europe, International History and German history in a transnational perspective. Recent publications: *Globale Vorherrschaft und Fortschrittsglaube: Europa 1850–1914* (Munich: C.H. Beck, 2019; Arabic transl.: Abu Dhabi: Kalima, 2022); *Cultural Sovereignty Beyond the Modern State: Space, Objects, and Media* (Berlin: De Gruyter Oldenbourg, with G. Feindt and B. Gissibl); *Gendering Global Humanitarianism in the Twentieth Century* (New York: Palgrave Macmillan, 2020; with E. Moeller and K. Stornig).

www.ingramcontent.com/pod-product-compliance
Lightning Source LLC
Chambersburg PA
CBHW050909300426
44111CB00010B/1451